M000116349

ARISE

DOREEN MOORE-BARRETT

ISBN 978-1-68517-994-6 (paperback)
ISBN 978-1-68517-995-3 (digital)

Copyright © 2021 by Doreen Moore-Barrett

All rights reserved. No part of this publication may be reproduced, distributed, or transmitted in any form or by any means, including photocopying, recording, or other electronic or mechanical methods without the prior written permission of the publisher. For permission requests, solicit the publisher via the address below.

Christian Faith Publishing, Inc.
832 Park Avenue
Meadville, PA 16335
www.christianfaithpublishing.com

Printed in the United States of America

This book is dedicated to my amazing and worthy husband, Levi. It's a privilege to share my success, joy, and love with you. You will never fully understand how much I honor you and how grateful I am that your support has withstood the test of time. I love you completely!

CONTENTS

Preface..7
Introduction..9
Life...13

Winter 17
    It's Working for Your Good.................................19
    Experience God's Unfailing Love 21
    Fearlessly Face the Unknown................................24
    From Test to Triumph 26
    Quiet and Confident Strength 30
    Rest in the Eye of the Storm................................32
    Strong When I Am Weak....................................37
    God Will Validate You 40
    It Has Come to Pass..43
    Isolation for Elevation 46
    Stay the Course...48

Spring 51
    From Ravaging to Restituting 53
    Time to Turn Around 56
    Season of Restoration..59
    Freed by the Power of Forgiveness 62
    A New Thing Awaits...66
    The Revived Remnant 68
    Trust Divine Providence......................................71
    The Becoming Season 73
    Unleash the Higher Order Thinking.....................75

Season of Appreciation...78
Stand Fast, It's Not Over Until It's Over...........................81
It's the Winnowing Season, What's Your Position?.............85

Summer! 89
Released to Be Refreshed...91
There Is a River...93
Season of Healing 95
It's Your Jubilee 98
Season of Dancing 101
A Ray of Hope...103
God Is Intentional About Your Life..................................105
The Cry That Touches the Heart of God 107
Join Force with the Covenant-Keeping God.....................109
Jesus, Rock in a Weary Land 111
Called to Conquer and Overcome 114
The Past Is Over 117
There Is No Condemnation..121
Say No to Mediocrity...126

Autumn..131
Season of Confidence..133
The Valley—Your Place of Restoration............................136
Be True to Your Calling..140
Embrace the Regenerated You! 143
Rise Above Fear...147
Bruised to Bless!...150
Turn Your Weeping into Worship 153
Beating Failure in the Second Round 158
"Speak the Word," Every Wall Must Fall 161
Understand the Inseparable Separation 164
Some Who Come Can't Go with You..................................167
You Will Sing the Victor's Song..170
The Storm Is Over 172

Conclusion...175

PREFACE

Life isn't a bed of roses. We all know that, right? Well, how much do we remember this fact when the storms of life begin to rage? What do we do when we don't know what to do?

Several persons have had many things to say.

- If you go ahead, Lord, I will follow…
- Though you slay me, I will trust you…
- I will arise and go to my Father…
- Entreat me not to leave thee…

Of course, those are only a few. But YOU, WHAT DO YOU SAY?

What did I say? I said I had, had enough! I said I couldn't cope any longer. I said that I was going to end it. I said I was going to rid this world of unnecessary trouble!

Yes, it was too much. The pains were excruciating, and living was meaningless. But that fateful day, I heard "ARISE!"

It wasn't spoken condescendingly. The voice wasn't loud, harsh, and accusatory. No, it was a soft whisper. It was almost as though I felt a gentle breath, which sent shivers through my body.

The voice held much promise as it had a captivating and endearing effect. It wasn't just another voice but the voice that changed my life.

I was lying on the floor where I had fallen asleep after praying once more. All along, I kept praying even when I knew it was only a matter of time before I ended my life. You see, nothing was changing, or at least that's how it seemed. But I didn't know what else to do, so I prayed. I was alive but dying.

That night I heard, "Fear not, for I am with you." Huh, who is this? I thought. Am I getting delusional? Am I losing my mind? I had no idea God spoke so audibly. Like Samuel, it was my first time hearing him for myself.

You guessed right! That night, over seventeen years ago, my life changed forever. Glory to God!

So who am I today? A vessel of honor saved by God's grace. I am a woman who has overcome many obstacles; walked through many valleys; climbed many mountains; and had battered knuckles, bruised knees, and deep cuts that Jesus Christ has gently cleaned and truly healed. As a result, I have a message for you! You are meant to live and not die!

This book isn't written by a victim but one who has bypassed the odds and today stands victorious. This book is designed for those who know they must, not might, overcome! This book is not a motivational one but one that is so anointed and invigorating that yokes will be broken in your life once you have read it.

INTRODUCTION

Dear friend, has it ever occurred to you that the situations you experience in your life may not be as much for you as the persons that you will meet on life's journey?

The book *Arise* was birth during a season of my life when I had enough challenges to keep me down. Being in a new region and attempting to integrate oneself can be challenging, on several levels, but through it all, God kept me strong. There were moments when I felt as though I wouldn't make it. A few times, I literally felt as though my world was crumbling, but then I discovered that all I needed to do, on any of those occasions, was to call on the name of the Lord, read His word, and stand on His promises. It was especially helpful to recall that he had never failed me in the past, so He wouldn't at that particular season.

Today, I can boast about the God of my salvation and let you know that he has become my song! Truly, I have learnt to lean and depend on him, and so can you. He assured me that my time of *jubilee* was fast approaching, and I did not doubt this because his words are truth and they are life. Since *jubilee* is represented by fifty years, I have written fifty short and inspiring stories, which I know will lead you to victory.

You are very important to God, and He wants you to know just how much through these pages. He wants you to know that no matter what has happened in your life, you were made by a very intentional, loving, and caring Father. It is He that made you. You are His child and are not meant to survive but to thrive.

So here is something, of which I wish to remind you, dearly beloved: It is your Father's good pleasure and delight that you grow in His grace and love. It is His will that your needs be met. He wishes above all else that you prosper and be in health, even as your soul prospers. There is one, however, that desires the very opposite for you. As much as is possible, therefore, he will leave no stone unturned until you are encompassed by troubles and filled with fears. He takes great delight in God's creation wandering around in misery and dejection. He hates you as much as God loves you, and his daily mission is to bring you to destruction. One of his many tools is *division*. Indeed, he knows that there is power in agreement, and so if two should stand together, he fights until they are divided. He knows that a divided house cannot stand. He is also cognizant that should he get you and me to be at odds, he stands a better chance of defeating the will and purpose of God for our lives. He knows that division is an effective way for people to embrace the spirit of rejection, which is good ground for bitterness, anger, strife, murder, and the ultimate destroyer—suicide. He knows that a spurned person is oftentimes a loner due to mistrust. Think, therefore, how much of a mastermind he is. This common enemy of our soul and all that is godly is the usurper—satan.

Having gone through many seasons in my life and being delivered, I know only too well how you feel from time to time. I have a message for you. This is a moment of deep intimacy, and I want you to understand that it isn't coincidental or by mere chance that you are holding this book. This was orchestrated for you before time began.

Do you remember when Jesus said to Peter, "Peter, Peter the devil desires to sift you like wheat but I have prayed for you! When you are strengthened, pray for your brethren!" Well, friend, that's exactly the reason why I wrote this book. Like you, I have experienced many troubles, and having been strengthened by the grace of God, it's time to strengthen you. I am confident that all portions of this book carry a profound message, which will bring healing and deliverance—not only to you but also to someone that you hold dear to your heart.

Please know that you are deeply loved, so much so that God took time to number every hair on your head. He has you on His mind, and there is not a day that goes by when He doesn't think about you. You are not and will never be forgotten. You can never exhaust God. Your concerns are of paramount importance to Him, which is why He instructed me to write this book.

I can't begin to tell you how grateful I am for His wisdom and council. Not one section of this book was written without divine enablement. I am truly thankful that He cares! I give Him praise today because He is truly a *repairer of the breach* (Isaiah 58:9–12). By the grace of this great God, I have included scriptures and a declaration at the end of every section. You shall be immensely blessed and shall overcome every trouble that seeks you as you meditate on and turn to the One who loves you more than anyone else can. May you never get to a place where you feel stuck, but if you do, remember something that you read here; it will help you to get on track again. May you never get to a place where you make the mistake of thinking that God doesn't love you. His love for you is unconditional, but at the same time, when He made you, He did with storms in mind. He knew your today would be like it is and your past the way it was. He has your future before Him, and there is nothing that can ever happen in your life to surprise or throw him into confusion.

As was mentioned earlier, He thought of you and always will. As these pages unfurl, you will get a better understanding of precisely to what I refer. As you read, seek a deeper relationship with God. If you haven't made Him your choice as yet, this is a good time to surrender your heart to Him. Allow the anointing of God to break every yoke as you read, in the mighty and exalted name, Jesus Christ of Nazareth! Shalom.

LIFE

Life is made up of times and season,
And for everything, there is a lesson and a reason.
Like a *winter* night cold and dark,
Some situations are drastic and, *oh*, very stark.
These are the lonesome, dismal, and desolate times,
When life throws darts, and you are tempted to scream and whine.
Then suddenly! Out of the gross dimness, nothingness, and gloom,
Comes your change like a light turned on in a dark room.
Causing the pains and agonies to dissipate and become a thing of the past,
For *spring* ushers in new hopes, dreams, and yes, victory at last.
Like a new flower, there is a bursting of destiny and a brand-new story,
And without warning, the sun begins to shine in all its glory.
With this season comes peace, happiness, and glorious bliss,
So much that even tears cannot prevent you from throwing God a kiss.
Even after many cold and dismal situations, you had no choice but to smile
Yes, some troubles were so much they seemed to stretch for many a long mile.
Some nights you went to bed, and due to affliction and oppression on every side,
You almost lost your mind and over the precipice of depression and insanity slide.

But at last *summer* came, filled with heat, warmth, and hope,
And after all was said and done, you realized there was no need for dope.
Now, in introspect, you recognize God gave you tenacity, inner strength, and wisdom;
And like a tree planted by the water, you are showing new growth and fresh blossom.
Life indeed came at you, with full force, and you were almost crushed,
But your purpose was to be manifested, and God was not to be rushed.
Well, when you thought it was as good as it could get, *autumn* finally came,
And like parched and dry ground, you started to experience the overflow of the rain.
Oh yes, no season remains forever, and like a tree, your circumstances are changing.
You who were once shunned and disdained are now in the peace of God radiating.
Yes; the kindling process is necessary and one that all experience; oh no, it's not a smooth sail!
But look at you glowing after you've come through and can now share your tale.
Indeed, the pain was real, daunting, and excruciating, and *yes!* The battering caused a shock,
But who would have known that today you would be as stable and solid as a rock.
Now you can encourage others to stay the course and finish well,
So they can strengthen others as their amazing story they tell.
After the winds, hails, sun, and rain, your life will bring God glory;
Many will be delivered, healed, and strengthened as you share your story,

Endure, therefore, hardness as a good soldier and don't try to short-circuit your preparation process,

For by and by, a life-changing testimony will come from all the sadness and the mess!

Winter

IT'S WORKING FOR YOUR GOOD

All butterflies have *complete metamorphosis*. To grow into an adult, they go through four stages: egg, larva, pupa, and adult. Each stage has a different goal. Depending on the type of butterfly, the life cycle may take anywhere from one month to a whole year.

Of all the stages of the butterfly, the pupa is the most remarkable for me. It is not fascinating because the term is close to *papa* but because the process is so unique. As soon as the caterpillar is done growing and has reached its full length and weight, it forms itself into a pupa, also known as a chrysalis. From the outside of the pupa, it looks as if the caterpillar may just be resting, but the inside is where all of the action is. Inside of the pupa, the caterpillar is rapidly changing.

What are you experiencing today? What situation are you going through? It could be that you are in your pupa stage. Perhaps this stage seems as if it's going to break you, but the truth is that it is only geared at making you. Your Lord wants you to be the perfect butterfly. You are not an ordinary butterfly, so do not settle for the mundane. He has a special assignment for you, and that's why you are having the experiences you are having.

Eat the good leaves on which you were born, and be sure to discard all leaves of discontent, self-pity, hate, and bitterness. You are a beautiful butterfly, and after your stages have expired, you will be seen, studied, and loved by all that cherish true beauty. Trust the process, and finish your course strong.

And we know that all things work together
for good to them that love God, to them who are
the called according to his purpose. (Romans 8:28)

Declaration

I am blessed, and I am a blessing. I am being molded on purpose, for purpose. All that is currently happening in my life and around me is for God's glory and my greater good.

EXPERIENCE GOD'S UNFAILING LOVE

The story of the prodigal son is a bittersweet one. It shows the love and forgiveness of a father, for his estranged son and the secret pains and bitterness harbored by the home-bound son. This story invokes a pungent feeling most times, especially if one is looking at the seemingly faithful son who remained at home while the prodigal left home and wasted his life.

For many years, I grappled with the unsettling feeling of unfairness when I read this story. I could not understand what the big deal was, concerning this very unscrupulous character who left home and created his demise. I felt great pity and even sympathy for the *faithful son* while my anger boiled at the foolishness of the father and the folly of his runaway son. Never once did it dawn on me, until much later, that this was a depiction of God's unfailing love for his alienated children. I observed that this youngster depicted the backslider and the elder son, those who are self-righteous, within the kingdom of God. They are the ones who have never exactly left home, or at least far from home. They have been faithful and appear as though their lives are intact.

For me, the essence of this story is not merely the conversion of the sinner, but in fact the restoration of an estranged believer into a good relationship with the Father. Oh, what wondrous love is depicted here? What amazing grace, patience, and tender mercies?

In this story, we see a father lovingly, patiently, and eagerly awaiting the return of his rebellious son. The story does not state how long this man looked in the distance on cool, balmy days, and during the shadows of the evening, but we see consistency in this message. We see long-suffering and the "forever I am married to you, oh, backslider" scenario unfurling! We see a demonstration of God's love for each individual and His attentiveness toward all humanity. We see also in this story, the benignancy of the father pursuing the sinfulness of the son.

My friend, from all indication, it is the memory of the father's goodness that brings the prodigal son to repentance. He remembered his father! He remembered his loving-kindness! He remembered his patience! His memories drove him to his knees and then to his feet! His memories of his father caused the gate of self-condemnation and rejection to swing wide open, thus causing his escape! The memory of his father's precious love took him from the pig's pen and navigated him home, where he truly belonged.

What does this story mean to you? Where are you now in your spiritual journey? Have you walked away from home, where you once held a place of pride and prestige? Have you walked away from the best thing that you ever had and are now experiencing untold pain and disgrace? Has sorrow and distress become your companion because of the decision you made? Have you walked away from the security and consolation of the Father's love? Is life throwing darts of destruction your way because you have moved away from the protection of the fold? Have you foolishly erred and walked away from your marriage? Are you stranded on the island of isolation due to a wrong business decision? Are you the black sheep of the family within which you were born?

Today can be your day! Today can be your acceptable day. The Father is looking for you. He is beckoning to you. He has not stopped loving you. Not one day has passed without Him hoping you would hear His voice and return to the fold. He continues to endure the glare of the sun as He looks in the distance for you. There are countless days when He has walked the old path, searching for you, even calling your name. Will you respond today? Will you allow yourself to experience true joy? He is standing at the door of your heart knocking. He is forever married to you. He, the potter, wants to put you back together again. *He* wants to reinstate you in business.

He wants to restore your marriage! He wants to assist you in making amends within your family circle.

Arise and come home! Leave the slum and malady of sin. Cease from allowing yourself to wallow in the pain of the past. Take action today! Arise and return to your Father! He specializes in the impossibilities of life. He will make wrong right. Go home, for Jesus is calling you. Go and enjoy the feast that awaits all those who return to the fold. Go home, my friend! Go home!

> I say unto you, that likewise joy shall be in heaven over one sinner that repenteth, more than over ninety and nine just persons, which need no repentance. (Luke 15:7)

Declaration

I am free from the pains and follies of my past! I rise from and escape the pit of rejection and confusion. I embrace the grace and mercies of my heavenly Father. I am free from all mistakes and setbacks. The glass ceiling of limitation that was over me is broken in the mighty name of Jesus Christ. I now walk into my God-ordained destiny, in Jesus's mighty name!

FEARLESSLY FACE THE UNKNOWN

Hey there, friend, as you are aware, there comes a point in every man's life when he must face the thing that he fears the most. Of course, this can be quite scary but is something that cannot be avoided. Indeed, this becomes quite critical, especially in the time within which we live. At least, we can prepare for the things we expect, but how do we prepare for the unexpected or the unseen?

One of the greatest challenges by which mankind has been plagued for many years is *fear of the unknown*. In his quest, therefore, to overcome this fear, man has gone far and wide to seek out the wise—sages and gurus. This mission has been relentless as he seeks to be provided with favourable and suitable news, which he hopes will, in turn, offer a safe harbor. The truth, however, is that God is the only one who truly knows the unknown because he lives in the unknown. He is shrouded by mystery and knows, fully well, the present, past, and future. Yes, He knows all things, but only to whom He chooses, does *He* reveal the deep mysteries of the ages.

My friend, from time to time, unknown circumstances will present themselves in your life. It is a given that no one knows what tomorrow holds. Despite this fact, God does not want you to live in fear. He has promised never to leave you alone.

When life gets scary because you have no idea what tomorrow holds, trust God! Move forward in boldness and understand that He, who canceled your past, knows your today and holds your tomorrow in his hand. The unknown is fully known to Him, and therefore, nothing takes him by surprise. Rest assured that he will never leave nor forsake you: This guarantee is for your elevation. This assurance is for the activation of your faith. Having this confidence that He, who has called you, can keep you—is enough to stimulate boldness and confidence. He will never fail nor forsake you. It doesn't matter what is happening in your life right now; trust God completely. Trust God wholeheartedly. Have faith in Him, and believe that He can deliver you from the darts of the wicked one. He will perfect that which concerns you. He will carry you over every mountain. He will bring you through every valley. Be still and know that He is God. Find boldness and courage in God. Trust Him, and you will not be disappointed.

> Take therefore no thought for the morrow:
> for the morrow shall take thought for the things
> of itself. Sufficient unto the day *is* the evil thereof.
> (Matthew 6:34)

Declaration

I am made perfect in love daily, so I free myself from all destructive thoughts of fear and doubt. I am confident that God will always take care of me. He will never leave nor forsake me. I, therefore, place my today and tomorrow in His capable hands.

FROM TEST TO TRIUMPH

> Life's a forge! Yes, and hammer and anvil, too! You'll be roasted, smelted, and pounded, and you'll scarce know what's happening to you. But stand boldly to it! Metal's worthless till it's shaped and tempered! More labor than luck. Face the pounding, don't fear the proving; and you'll stand well against any hammer and anvil. (Lloyd Alexander, *Taran Wanderer*)

So what does it mean "to be tested in life," dear friend?

Most times we are challenged when asked this question. The answer varies, and yet as hard as we try, most of us believe and even act as though tests are geared at destroying us!

The reality, however, is that tests are for our good. Scriptures reveal that when we have been tested and tried, we shall come forth as pure gold. So again, what is a test and how does God test us? It is quite simple: When a believer comes into a relationship with God, both of them enter a spiritual covenant. Yes, the believer and God agree. As the covenant is entered, God assesses the resolve of this person by giving him or her physical, spiritual, mental, emotional difficulties to overcome. In other words, when a person publicly states at the time of surrendering his life to Jesus that he has forsaken all to follow Him, he is indefinitely renouncing the old way of life and stating quite clearly that he is embracing a new walk and lifestyle. As such, the individual starts the new journey; then Christ, now his Master teacher, begins to teach and lead him into the path of righteousness (Psalm 23:3). What the believer does not understand most times is that the Lord does these tests to provide a way for him or her to bring glory to His name.

Indeed, the sinner is now a saint being taught the necessary steps to overcome the old life and embrace the new. You could jolly well say, the saint is now in a boot camp, or if you want to make it milder, he is now in rehabilitation to be detoxed from sin and learn holiness. This, however, is not a robotic situation because the Holy Spirit, who is the Comforter, whilst desirous of bringing peace to this individual, during this moment of testing, knows and allows conscious choice on his or her part.

My friend, all you need to know is this—who you are in Christ Jesus and who *He* is to you. You see, God is not just your Creator but is desirous of being your Master Teacher, Confidant, and Friend. As you know, teachers test their students after teaching them different lessons. The teacher does not test the child because he hates the child, but in fact, because he wants to see what the child is learning or has learnt.

The test has a twofold duty: On one hand, it serves as a way to judge the student based on merit. On the other hand, it determines the knowledge of the learner. Without conducting tests, the student doesn't concentrate on his studies and learn his lessons properly. Tests are therefore necessary in life to find out one's true skills, talents, and knowledge. Likewise, tests in the life of the believer do not only determine the reward but help the child to understand the next step or level he must take or go.

Indeed, friend, I fully agree with you that most of us do not enjoy being tested. We take great pleasure in life when everything is going smoothly, but when a storm begins to brew, we begin to quake within. We fail to remember that smooth seas do not cultivate (make) skillful sailors. Testing in life is beneficial because as our faith is tested, it produces patience in us. We can all say that we are believers, but unless we pass the four main tests of life, similar to those experienced by Abraham, we will not be suitable for the kingdom of God. The four tests to our faith are the following:

1. *A Major Change. Heb*rew 11:8 says, "By faith, Abraham when he was called to go to a place he would later receive as his inheritance, obeyed and went even though he did not know where he was going."

2. *A Delayed Promise.* Hebrews 11:9 says, "By faith, Abraham made his home in the promised land like a stranger in a foreign country and he lived in tents as did Isaac and Jacob who were heirs with him of the same promise." God wants us to base our lives on promises, not on explanations but expectations. What He told Abraham was, "If you move, I will give you the land of Israel." The problem is, after he got there, there was a delay in the transfer of ownership. Even after living one hundred more years, Abraham still had not received the promise.

3. *An Impossible Problem.* If you are a believer, in your lifetime, God will put you up against an impossible problem. Hebrews 11:11–12 says, "By faith, Abraham, even though he was past age, and Sarah herself was barren, was enabled to become a father because he considered Him faithful who had made the promise…" As good as God's promise was, there was a minor problem because, at age ninety-nine, Abraham still didn't have any kids.

4. *A Senseless Tragedy.* The ultimate test. The test that causes us to ask, "Why?" Hebrews 11:17–19 says,

> By faith, Abraham, when God tested him he offered Isaac as the sacrifice. He who had received the promise was about to sacrifice his one and only son. Even though God had said to him, "it's through Isaac that your offspring will be reckoned." Abraham reasoned that God could raise

the dead and figuratively speaking he did receive
Isaac back from the dead.

So, my friend, what more can I say? No matter what you are experiencing today, rest assured that God will see you through. The teacher will always be quiet as his student is tested. If you feel as though God is quiet as you are tested, trust the process and remain fearlessly faithful. Know also that as long as you are walking in obedience to *His* will and purpose for your life, all things will work together for your good. Press forward, and in due course, you shall be rewarded

> But He knows the way that I take [and He pays attention to it]. *When* He has tried me, I will come forth as [refined] gold [pure and luminous]. (Job 23:10 AMP)

Declaration

I am focused, alert, and aware that tests are inevitable in life. I am a possessor of the Issachar's anointing. I know the season and time within which I live. I am getting better every day as I am learning the ways of my heavenly Father. I triumph over every trial, in the exalted name, Jesus Christ of Nazareth!

QUIET AND CONFIDENT STRENGTH

Hey, friend, have you ever noticed the standards by which persons are evaluated many times?

In a world where the hype has become a new norm, you may feel like a misfit—when you are not of a loud and brawling persona. Many people are seen as stupid or shallow if they are *quiet*. This is not necessarily the case, however, as these are the ones who often possess great confidence and strength. Without prejudice or fear, I dare to say that *nothing*, and I mean absolutely nothing, is wrong with you being a strong, quiet type of person who carries yourself differently. In fact, I appreciate, on a greater level, a presence that demonstrates both strength and humility at the same time rather than a proud body who proves to be only an empty braggart.

If the truth is to be told, beloved, a person of few words is not necessarily one that is challenged, where speech is concerned. Such an individual has possibly learnt to master an art many are still battling with, the art of overtalking. At times we judge a book by the cover, but we have missed the mark in many cases. A quiet and confident person is a strong one, one who was likely tested by various circumstances in life, succeeded, and saw no reason to brag about such occurrences.

So let's break down what I am saying. When I refer to quiet, I mean a humble person, and by strength, I mean a physical presence that is not referring to your size. A quiet and confident person who shows strength may also be categorized as one who knows how to handle success without boasting. There is more to life than showing off, which is a foolish person's glory. Much more is achieved every time in quiet and confidence. People with these attributes are balanced and understand how to exercise resilience in tough times. This is called exercising grace under pressure.

A quiet and confident person is not governed by a proud and dominating spirit that turns others off, as it is laced by haughtiness. People who are quiet and confident understand that if they are strong or gaining momentum, they should maintain a level head and not allow themselves to be overtaken by conceit, which is an open door for the devil. These people detest flattery and every form of attention-seeking. They enjoy calling attention to the accomplishments and achievements of others. The simple truth is that they do not get a kick by praising themselves.

Finally, being quiet and confident isn't about shining a lamp on yourself but being on a mission to illuminate the way, as best as possible, to lead others to shine as they should.

> Thus saith the LORD, Let not the wise man glory in his wisdom, neither let the mighty man glory in his might, let not the rich man glory in his riches. (Jeremiah 9:23)

Declaration

I am comfortable in the reality that the One who made me knows my going out and coming in. I will therefore remain quiet and confident, knowing full well that pride is folly while humility is a great treasure!

REST IN THE EYE OF THE STORM

As the storm clouds swirled angrily across the sky, the young expectant mother peeked in her cupboard and shakily whispered the dreaded words to her husband, "We are not prepared, hon. We have used up all but two candles, and the nonperishable supplies are very low. Should this storm last for very long, we will be in a terrible state. I know the meteorologist had said a storm was pending, but I didn't believe it. As a result, I made no preparation."

As his wife whispered those words from her quivering lips, he peered at her in sympathy and not without some irritation. As a sailor, he knew he had been absent for a good portion of her pregnancy. This was because his job, though not taking preeminence in his life, was important. It was his livelihood, and he was the main breadwinner. He knew the life he desired for his family, and he had, as much as he could, always ensured that her every need was met.

Life was good so far, and he was able to secure a maid for her, even as they had scheduled several interviews for a wet nurse who would aid his wife over the first few months after childbirth. He certainly wanted things to be in order. He wasn't trying to replace himself, but he planned to ensure that his darling was as comfortable as could be in the final trimester of her pregnancy. Having taken a long leave of absence, he had arrived home barely escaping the tail of the storm, which was now battering the house mercilessly. He was quite weary, and the greatest desire of his heart was to shower, eat a quick supper, and cuddle his wife. This woeful tale was not what he expected to hear at all. He knew this was their first child, and he was jubilant. It's true that his wife was a good woman, notwithstanding a bit fickle at times, but unprepared in a storm, which was not a small one at that?

What was he going to do? Even as she looked at him, he could hear the deep rumble in the background, accompanied by lightning blazing across the sky. The rain battering across the windowpane was certainly not very encouraging.

Not only were they not prepared for the storm, but she was heavy with child. He knew that anything could happen over the next few hours, and their nearest neighbor was half mile away. For the first time, he realized the magnitude of their dilemma.

Well, my friend, that storyline might only pique your interest on the basis that it is a good read, but there is much to be garnered from it. How truly prepared are we for the storms of life? How ready are we when the challenging moments come our way? How do we prepare for storms?

Just as there are atmospheric storms, there are storms that assail our lives at different times. Unlike atmospheric storms, physical, emotional, financial, and even mental storms often hit without warning. They don't usually announce themselves in advance, and a lot of times, we are totally unprepared for the upheaval that they cause when they come along.

Where I am from, there is a proverb that says, "A *young bird* does *not know storm.*" Meaning: *Young* people are more carefree and are *not* aware of the dangers of life. Indeed, that is true, but there are tons of middle age and older folks who are simply not prepared for the *storms* of life. This is because many have testified and continue to testify that at various times, adverse circumstances hit them without warning. I can personally attest to the fact that sometimes it was when I was struck by a certain adversity that I recognized what had really happened.

Believe me, friends, it's not that you are oblivious, but there are times when a storm is so subtle that it creeps up unaware. It takes the grace of God and a discerning spirit to acknowledge the very depth of this storm.

So what are life's storms? You may wonder why I waited so long to ask, but it is deliberate! For you to navigate this journey called life, you must fully understand what are storms, the three types, and how to ride out your storm by God's grace. In brief, you must and will need to know how to rest in the eye of the storm.

According to one source, a storm is any disturbed state of a body especially affecting its surface and strongly implying a wind-force. It may be marked by significant disruptions and lightning (a thunderstorm), heavy precipitation (snowstorm, rainstorm), heavy freezing rain (ice storm), strong winds (tropical cyclone, windstorm), or wind transporting some substance through the atmosphere as in a dust storm, blizzard. Well, as you are aware, my friend, even in a storm, there is a safe haven. This is called the eye of the storm. It is, in fact, the calm region at the center of a storm.

Every human being experiences storms in his lifetime. It is so certain that even as I write this book, there are millions, including yourself who may be going through a storm, will be going through one, or has just exited a storm. Yes, my friend, there are three types of storms: *those we cause or create, those created by others, and finally those created and caused by God.*

The first storm I will look at is the storm that Jonah caused in his own life. This began brewing when he allowed disobedience to lead him in the opposite of his God-given direction. We saw him being cast overboard the ship on which he was hidden. Things got to a climax when we later learnt that he was not just trashing around in the water, for dear life, but found himself face-to-face with all the messy contents of a whale's stomach. What a storm?

Let's now examine another storm, this one experienced by Joseph. Wow! What a colorful life this fellow lived? It makes sense that he received a coat of many colors from his dad because it, among other things, symbolized his escapades in life! So what was Joseph's trouble? He was surrounded by jealous brothers and even at one time a loving but confused dad, one who questioned the meaning of his dream! As if members of his own family were not skeptical and hated him enough, Joseph's life spiraled out of control after his brothers placed him into a pit, then removed and sold him to traveling merchants.

Over an unmentioned period in his new place of residence, Egypt, Joseph operated in freedom. Before he knew it, however, he was making an athletic dash to escape a major act of adultery staged by his master's wife. Soon he found himself placed into prison, but *finally* he rose to the highest position in that strange land. Talk about turbulence! What a stormy life? We know that all things work for good to them that love God and are called. Indeed, Joseph's storms caused by everyone else but himself were nerve-racking, but he did survive them all!

The final storm, to which I will draw your attention, is the one that occurred in the life of Job. His was quite tempestuous and went on for an extended period. You see, my friend, this storm could not be measured by a meteorologist, but everything called normalcy was blown from his life. He, who was once a most affluent, organized, and well-respected prince, was reduced to a childless, poverty, worm-matted, lonely, and desperate bag of bones. Was he the cause of this storm? No, it was a storm allowed by God, because he was in the throes of one of the most vicious tests ever experienced by any human being. Yes, my friend, this was a storm staged by satan but allowed by God.

Having read all the scenarios above, we can conclude that God is the greatest! He can and will calm any and every storm. He will calm them once we cry out to Him in prayer. He will come to our rescue.

My friend, I have experienced various storms in my life. While I thought that I would have been destroyed, they have all helped my growth and development. I can't begin to tell you how I have mustered strength from crying out to God and also patiently resting in Him.

What storms face you today, dearest one? Are you experiencing whirlwind-like situations that appear to be sucking you in? Are there cyclones that are beating against you physically, emotionally, socially, financially, or even spiritually? Do you feel as though you will not survive life's blows that are being meted at you? Cry out to Jesus! He is the peace speaker! He is mighty to save. He is merciful. He is gracious and kind! He will help you, even if you are the cause of your own storm! He will stand by and support you against the onslaught of all human-incited storms! Call His beautiful and life-changing name! Breathe that name in prayer! I assure you that as this occurs, slowly or even instantaneously, you will notice the calm! I give you Jesus today because when everything and everyone fails: He will support you to the very end! Look to Him, and make Him your bridge. He will carry you across, and you will smile again.

> But now thus saith the LORD that created thee, O Jacob, and he that formed thee, O Israel, Fear not: for I have redeemed thee, I have called *thee* by thy name; thou *art* mine. When thou passest through the waters, I *will be* with thee; and through the rivers, they shall not overflow thee: when thou walkest through the fire, thou shalt not be burned; neither shall the flame kindle upon thee. (Isaiah 43:1–2)

Declaration

I embrace the peace of God. I decree and declare that I am an overcomer and therefore cannot be defeated by life's storms! No matter how boisterous are the circumstances around me, I will rest in Jesus, the eye of the storm!

STRONG WHEN I AM WEAK

The grasslands and forests are filled with wildlife of all sorts and sizes. The largest animals are the elephants. Elephants are a *keystone* of species. If such species get extinct, the entire ecosystem would change drastically. The reason for this is because other species rely on the keystone species for survival.

Elephants are highly intelligent and emotionally complex animals. They also have a unique buildup. There are more than one hundred thousand muscle units in their trunk, making them sensitive enough to pick up objects as small as a penny and strong enough to lift a whole tree. An elephant's trunk is the fusion of its upper lip and nose and is absolutely flexible serving as a nose, an arm, a hand, a voice, and much more. Elephants favour either their left or right tusk, just as people favour one hand over the other.

Did you know, however, that despite their sizes, they are weaker in comparison to many small creatures? I know, I know. I was taken aback myself. Take for example ants, which measure between 0.75 and 52 millimeters! These small animals are well known for their united work ethics, agility, strength, and endurance. According to studies, executed by scientists, they use different parts of their bodies effectively, but their compound eyes with multiple lenses enable them to see clearly small particles with different colors.

Unlike the elephant and other animals, by putting into practice information that is collected by their antennae and eyes, ants are able to work day and night. It is even more shocking to see ants pass with heavy loads on their mouth. They are able to lift up and move a cargo, which weighs five hundred times more than their body weight. These animals are equipped with flexible and powerful mandibles, which work perfectly like an elephant's trunk. This is possible because an ant is able to apply a bite with pressure measuring more than five thousand times its body weight. Among the species of ants, some are capable of carrying weight between 350 and 1,000 times their body weight. Oh yes, though small in size and seemingly powerless, God has made ants able to execute tasks that exceed their sizes.

What about you today, my friend? What is your strength? What is your size? Do you spend quality time comparing yourself to others? Do you waste your days thinking about the things that seem difficult and impossible? Do you know that God's strength is available to you? Do you know that He has given you power over the power of the enemy? *Yes*, there is a God who is well able! You can do any impossible task through Him *who gives you the power to take action*.

Despite how you feel and though your strength may be small right now, begin to activate your faith! Open your mouth and speak life over yourself, your household, and all that pertains to you. Look unto Jesus Christ! You are meant to be a fortified city of God. Allow Him to be that Rock and Fortress on which you stand. He wants to be or remain your God. He won't leave you alone. You feel alone only because you are focusing on the trouble. Turn your attention away from the physical, and tap into the spiritual. Begin to worship God, and see how your burdens become light.

> And he said unto me, "My grace is sufficient for thee: for my strength is made perfect in weakness. Most gladly therefore will I rather glory in my infirmities, that the power of Christ may rest upon me." (2 Corinthians 12:9)

Declaration

As I abide in and rely on the grace of God, my strength is renewed as the eagle. I face every difficulty with confidence knowing that my battles are not won by my strength nor might but by the spirit of the Lord. Amen.

GOD WILL VALIDATE YOU

Human relationship is the core of life in every strata of society. The most critical or core ingredient that enhances and cements any healthy and thriving relationship is trust. The foundational building block of a healthy team is trust. Without trust, social units are different collections of individuals waiting to fall apart. While various factors lead to mistrust, some of the most crucial ones include a failure to keep promises, agreements, and commitments made, the demonstration of an inconsistency between what is said and what is done, the tendency to serve self first and others only when it is convenient, and a failure to be truthful.

Well, friend, surely we are human, and we aren't perfect, right? Regarding this matter, there can be no debate, however, for many people, the bone of contention is not merely the factors mentioned above but the way they are dealt with. Where there is an overdrive of arrogant and selfishness, one can hardly see his or her wrongs, much less, a reason to show regret and remorse. Where these factors are concerned, there is bound to be an escalation of the problem and, finally, the bursting of the balloon.

So the question is, "How do I know that you are who you say you are?" How do I know that I can trust you? How do I verify your authenticity and legitimacy? These are questions that continue to be asked by the masses, and no one is exempted. From the pope to the pauper, the eyes of scrutiny are opened, and many people have become and continue to be distrustful of all and sundry!

Why is this so? What has happened to cause such a sad malady? Sin is the case of dishonesty, suspicions, and every form of facades.

Sin and the manifestation of its accompanying sons, *lies* and *deception*, are the cause of all kinds of mistrust! Since the birth of these brothers, everyone has developed questioning minds because he has been swindled or deceived at one point or another. Do we have to doubt everything though? Is it as bad as it seems? The answers will vary and range from humorous to horrifying, but the reality is that for many, the proof of the pudding can and will only be determined once it is eaten!

While the world is filled with webs of confusion, deception, and lies, we will do well to understand that not all people are evil. There is still a remnant that has pledged to remain authentic and connected with honesty and integrity. Indeed, it is appalling and disheartening to recognize that things are the way they are. This, however, is another of the many reflections of sin. It is a sure sign that due to his depravity, shame, and disgrace, man has become another being. Mankind has changed from truth to fraud and corruption.

So in the meantime, based on the system of the world and the atrocious behavior of many that has left quite a bad taste of distrust, will you be upset when someone mistrusts or questions your validity? Or will you understand their standpoint and prove the doubters wrong? Yes, you can.

Again to each, his own might be the easiest thing to say. But what do you do when deep down, you are certain you are a true witness of the Light, your Lord and Savior Jesus Christ? You can only do this one thing: remain true to the cause you represent. Stop trying to defend yourself. Don't argue, fuss, or fight. Continue to be focused, and God will prove the truth that you bear!

> And the woman said to Elijah, now by this I know that thou art a man of God, and that the word of the LORD in thy mouth is truth. (1 Kings 17:24)

Declaration

I am a truth bearer! The word of God shall not only defend but also vindicate me. It is my shield and buckler. He shall cause me to triumph over every lie of the cohorts of hell.

IT HAS COME TO PASS

Don't let go of that thread of hope. Sometimes life happens. Sometimes things become chaotic, and yes, it does appear as though all hope is gone, but guess what, friend? No season lasts forever! Every season has a set duration *of time*. Take for example, spring, it is a beautiful time for many people, especially nature lovers. Spring announces its arrival with new birth, growth, and warm sunshine. During this season, it even appears as though there is a rebirth since trees that shed their leaves begin to send out new leaves and very soon they start to blossom. Grass that was covered under the mounds of snow begin to show forth their blades, and even the birds begin to chirp. As amazing as this season is, does it last forever? *No, it doesn't!*

Even summer, which comes with a prevailing heat and much warmth (on many levels), go swiftly accompanied by autumn, with its many colors, and then comes winter. This is the coldest and most devastating season, but does it last forever? No, it doesn't—it comes and it passes. Winter comes, and undoubtedly, its presence is felt and heard. This is because it is generally accompanied by wind, snow, sleet, and rain. As bad as things are during that time, we all know that it, as with all other seasons, only comes to pass!

As are the seasons in the earth's atmosphere, so are the days of our lives. Everything has an appointed time, and nothing lasts forever. So what am I trying to say to you, who are currently reading this page? No matter how bad things are right now, no matter how adverse they seem, they have come, but they too will pass. Do you think you'll be crying forever? The devil is a liar! Do you think that you'll be hurting forever? That news you received, that diagnosis from the doctor, that bank statement that is causing your heart to palpitate to the point of near or possible panic, that attack on your marriage, that attack on your ministry or even your mind, your reputation which is under siege or even your integrity, which may be under fire, has come *to pass*! Yes, it's frustrating; yes, it's overwhelming. Who would dare to tell you that it's not painful? Certainly not me. The reality, however, is that I know the God who neither slumbers nor sleeps.

Perhaps you know Him as Master yourself but are currently feeling alone. Maybe you have never had a personal relationship with Him, but whatever the case is: He is real! *He* loves and cares for His creation, and you can bet your last dime on the truth that He will never fail nor forsake His own.

It's true that weeping endures for a night, but joy comes in the morning. Do you know why your weeping can never be permanent? God is a promise keeper, and one of his promises to you is that you will be a recipient of beauty for the ashes of pain, abuse, rejection, past hurts, offense, sicknesses, and diseases, and all that has ever ailed you. He will give you strength for every fear you have ever experienced—the oil of joy for mourning and peace for despair. He wants you to embrace the truth that your trial comes not to stay but to pass!

Whatever storms are brewing and whatever category of force they come with shall not uproot you if you seek shelter in the Rock of All Ages. His name is Jesus! He will see you through. He will heal you. He will save you from your distress, and you will laugh again. Look up today. Friend, please understand that if you are already down, the only place to look is up. This too shall pass. Look unto Jesus. He is the author and finisher of your *faith*. He is faithful, and He never fails. Give glory to your Creator, and let Him have His way in you, in Jesus's *holy* and matchless name.

> For I will restore health unto thee, and I will
> heal thee of thy wounds, said the LORD; because
> they called thee an Outcast, saying, this *is* Zion,
> whom no man seek after. (Jeremiah 30:17)

Declaration

Nothing in life is permanent including pains, hardship, sorrows, and distress. I have a yet praise! I rejoice in sorrow because still I rise! Everything that is currently causing me pain and confusion shall cause me to emerge into my purpose, in the *mighty name* of Jesus Christ of Nazareth!

ISOLATION FOR ELEVATION

David, more than anyone else, knew the betrayal of friends, family members, and associates alike. He understood what the paths of loneliness and isolation entailed. He spent long periods in the desert, under the canopy of the skies. During those times, his only companions were his sheep and his harp, which made his heart merry. He fought lions and bears alone. In the heat of battle, he, through the power of God, conquered the Philistine giant, Goliath, who was a terror to the nation of Israel. During the aftermath of war, when he should be relaxing and basking in post-victory jubilee, he had to run for his life as King Saul sought his life day and night.

Let down by friends, he lived a lonely life and seemingly sought love in the wrong places a few times. As if that was not enough, his son, Absalom, whom he loved dearly, rose against him. For years, David had little peace. He lived the life of a refugee, fleeing the very ones he served. He loved God, yet he made mistakes, wrong decisions, and sinned against *Him* in ways that he shouldn't, but God was the only constant in his life.

He found solace in knowing that God was not a man and that He loved him (David) despite his faults, failings, and shortcomings. David found peace and fullness of joy in God's presence. To many, David's Psalms might sometimes appear paradoxical, but we cannot deny that though many of them reflect pains and sadness; we see the pen of an articulate and confident subduer flashing across the pages of time. We see the inner strength of a man who battled life and overcame it. Though we see words reflecting pains and desolation, these are accompanied by words of deep hope and repose.

We can safely say therefore that David lived a fulfilled life because his confidence was in God. It's no wonder that at one time he penned the following words: "I have been young and now I am old but I have never seen the righteous forsaken…" David's confidence led to several seasons of comfort in God. Those were days and nights when, despite the tears that flowed from his eyes, he openly declared that God was his very present help, God was the hill from whence his help came. God was a Rock for him, in a weary land. These and many such words caused us to realize that David sought and drew comfort from the Word and presence of God.

What are you experiencing today? What difficulty have you been attempting to endure? Are you shackled by a heavy burden? Are you cumbered with a load of care? Jesus wants to take your burdens. He is saying, "Cast your cares upon me; I care for you." He is saying, "Come, let us reason together. Though your sins are as scarlet, they shall be as white as snow though they are red as crimson, they shall be made like wool." He is calling you today. He is saying to you, "Come, my child: I want to dress your wound. I want to pour the oil and wine within. I want to make you whole." Are you broken inside? Are you bruised? Are you covered by layers of pain concealers? Jesus is waiting. He's the good shepherd.

> Thou shall increase my greatness, and com-
> fort me on every side. (Psalm 71:21)

Declaration

God is my strength and my song. He has become my salvation. He is my portion! He is within me, and no weapon formed against me shall prosper. This too shall pass by the power of the Lord Jesus Christ.

STAY THE COURSE

Hey, friend, how many times have you watched your favorite sports personality as his picture was captured in the grandstand or arena? How excited have you been each time you watched, with bated breath and pounding heart, as he took his place behind the starting block? Did you find that you could barely contain yourself as you anxiously looked on, even measuring and calculating mentally, the likelihood of the other athletes, prevailing against him as he barreled to the finish line? Well, hopefully, you can relate to that because I have had several of those moments. To be quite frank, I always have a hard time suppressing my glee as my champion reaches the finish line.

But stop! Has it ever occurred to you that the said sprinter comes under various attacks and challenges during training and even while running? Has it ever dawned on you that he encounters but overcomes many obstacles to achieve the medal he so deservedly collects each time?

Let's look at nature. What of the beautiful lotus blossom, which is a type of water lily. Do you understand how it grows? Did you know that the roots of the lotus blossom are grounded in the mucky, muddy bottoms of ponds and lakes? Wait a moment, because I'm not sure you heard my question, let's ask again. Did you know that the lotus must grow upward through mud and dirty water until it eventually reaches the surface to bloom into a bright, exceptionally beautiful flower? Oh yes, my friend, it is the ability of the lotus flower to brave the darkness and murkiness and still become something so immaculate and exquisite that makes it something so very special to many plant lovers.

My friend, for you to enjoy the prize, you must stay the course! If you hope to reap the benefit of success, you must be prepared to endure the teething pains that accompany the journey. You must be prepared to enjoy the rough-and-tumble ride that accompanies attainment. You must be able to survive both hot summers and cold winters. You must understand that real winners endure the drought when rainfall is scarce in their area. Winners know with all certainty that they will bloom even in the late season, so they must stay the course!

My friend, life is a battle, but if you are determined and trust wholeheartedly in God, you will achieve your goals regardless of obstacles or negative criticism. You will keep going strongly to the end of the race. Yes, there may be an early setback in the first half, but if you stay the course, you will reap your reward.

My friend, coupled with endurance must be a strong belief in yourself that no matter what your circumstances may be, no matter how dark and murky things may seem outside, perfection is already within you. During those times, you have to trust God and call to remembrance your God-given potential. Yes, my friend, believe in your beauty and goodness. Stay the course, and you will, undoubtedly, blossom and illuminate the light within you.

> And thine ears shall hear a word behind thee, saying, this is the way, walk ye in it, when ye turn to the right hand, and when ye turn to the left. (Isaiah 30:21)

Declaration

I am a possessor of great endurance. No matter how difficult a situation is, I will never waver from my God-given goals. I will stay my course and blossom in every area of my life.

FROM RAVAGING TO RESTITUTING

Hello there, friend, did you know that many folks who appear and even sound happy are, in fact, truly desperate and longing for healing and deliverance?

In the Gospel of Luke, we read a story of sheer amazing grace. As this narrative unfurls, we meet a "not very nice or pleasant" character in the person of Zacchaeus. If you understand the history of that era, tax collectors made the lives of the average populous extremely difficult. They taxed heavily and unsympathetically. The problem with Zacchaeus was that he wasn't just a tax collector but the chief one in his region, Jericho of Judea. Being a citizen of Judea, he was expected to have mercy on his people, but he had become very corrupt and oppressive, thus attracting much hatred to himself.

It appears that the Romans found pleasure in hiring locals such as Zacchaeus to collect money from their people. In exchange, these tax collectors pledged their allegiance to Rome and charged a high commission for their job. They also took a little skimming off the top for themselves, which is why they were gravely hated!

Being the chief of this corruption made Zacchaeus wealthy and powerful. It doesn't require much to see that he wasn't well-liked because he was seen as a gluttonous traitor.

Friend, you must bear in mind that when an individual is used to doing dirty work, he is really not well-liked. Even the person who's using him resents him most times. It is only a matter of time before such individual is eradicated if the opportunity presents itself.

Zacchaeus appeared to be a lonely man. When it was noised abroad that Jesus was in the area, no one prepared a platform for him. Not even his counterparts seemed to be around, and his best alternative to seeing Jesus was to climb a sycamore tree.

To the chagrin of the crowd, Jesus did not only look in the direction of this villain but invited himself to his house. What! Are you kidding me? How could He, who claimed to be the Son of God, not know that this man was a thief? Is this for real, they wondered? Who has ever heard of such madness? Jesus proved them all wrong. He showed on that day the very reality of His entry to this world, to save those that are lost.

At the amazing grace of the loving Savior, Zacchaeus's heart, which was hardened overtime by greed and deceit, melted, and oh, what a saving experience for one so lost? Mercy that day was great, and grace was free; pardon there was multiplied to this man: Because of his experience, he openly declared, "Behold, Lord, the half of my goods I will give to the poor; and if I have taken anything from any man by false accusation, I restore him fourfold."

Through Jesus Christ, restitution can happen. Through the efficacious blood of Jesus Christ, the vilest sinner can be made clean. In his day, Zacchaeus promised to return fourfolds to those he robbed. What have you lost, or did you by any chance take something you shouldn't have? Jesus makes the difference! He renews, refreshes, and restores.

The forgiveness Jesus gave was not just meted out to Zacchaeus but his entire household, and friend, the efficaciousness of the blood is still bringing healing and enforcing restitution. It is still available for everyone who desires it today. Like Zacchaeus, salvation can come to you, right now, for the Son of Man came to seek and to save the lost.

> Forbearing one another and forgiving one another, if any man has a quarrel against any: even as Christ forgave you, so also do ye. And above all these things put on charity, which is the bond of perfectness. (Colossians 3:13–14)

Declaration

Today, I embrace the forgiveness of Jesus Christ and the power of His healing virtue. I surrender my will and my ways to His dictate and decree and declare that I will never be the same again, in Jesus's *mighty* name!

TIME TO TURN AROUND

Have you ever been at a low place spiritually, or better yet, are you currently at a low place? A place which you may have gotten to or is currently at that has caused you to be engulfed with feelings of hopelessness and despair? Have you ever found yourself in or are you presently experiencing a wilderness situation, as a result of doing your own thing? Have you ever felt as though you were in the belly of a whale, kind of like Jonah, because you tried to escape the route God wanted you to take? Do you know what I am talking about? Maybe not, huh! (Chuckling.)

Perhaps that has never been your story, but quite a few people, including myself, have had such an experience at one point or another of our lives. During those crushing moments, it seemed as though all hope was lost, and God had no further use or purpose for me. In fact, if you are a person that truly loves God, you will soon discover that your conscience goes into overdrive once you go against the will of God.

These are the moments during which emotions run wild, and we have many restless days and sleepless nights. Of course, as human beings, we are subjected to passions and emotions, and that's when the guilt, the feeling of loss and sorrow, becomes almost too much to bear. This is because we know we have sinned and come short of God's glory. These are also the moments during which the old dragon, satan, begins his cruel whispering, "Shut up! Be quiet, you've sinned, and there is no use to pray. God has no further use for your kind." These are the times when you must be on your double watch for the spirits of rejection and condemnation. Such demons are assigned to continue the taunting and mockery of their master. They aim to cause you to remain in a place of stagnancy and derision.

If you don't understand the operations of the enemy of your soul, and if you don't fully grasp the Father's love, you will find yourself sinking into the mire of rejection and self-condemnation. This is an abyss you want to escape as you don't want to lose your identity. You don't want to become a hardened and loveless individual who, if not helped, get on to a path of self-destruction even destroying others on the journey.

My friend, my dear friend, this is a good time to embrace the Father's love. This is a time to become broken before the Potter, thus recognizing that there is hope for you. He loves you with an everlasting love. As Master Potter, He takes pleasure in remaking marred vessels. It is *His* good pleasure to mold and make you new.

You may feel alone in the battles of life. The old liar may be telling you right now that you've sinned, and there's no possibility of you turning around, but guess what? If you will seek the Lord and confess your sin to *Him*: He is willing to forgive you.

You see, friend, this was also the Jew's story. They had fallen into transgression and had erred because of a lack of the Word. I believe, you know, that the less time we spend in the word is the weaker we become, thus making ourselves easy prey for the enemy.

In their case, the day Nehemiah imparted this precious commodity, they were heavily convicted and began to weep. They were sure there was no redemption for them, but Nehemiah reminded them that "the joy of the Lord was their strength."

Jesus is your Redeemer and Savior. He wants to give hope and new life to you, despite your shortcomings. It is His good pleasure that your tears become laughter and your sorrows turn to joy. Friend, no matter how things look, when you turn to God, He turns things around. You can rely on His infallible Word! You can trust Him to turn your mourning into dancing. He is well able! This is a good time to turn around. Approach Him boldly, humbly, and truthfully, and He will turn things around. He never despises a broken and contrite heart, and He will certainly not turn you away. Seek Him while He is near, and call upon Him while He can be found.

> If my people, which are called by my name, shall humble themselves, and pray, and seek my face, and turn from their wicked ways; then will I hear from heaven, and will forgive their sin, and will heal their land. (2 Chronicles 7:14)

Declaration

I overcome all weaknesses by the power of the blood of Jesus Christ of Nazareth! Today I choose redemption over rejection. I choose conviction over condemnation. I am a child of God knowing fully well that fallen doesn't mean unrestorable! It's my season of turning around and pursuing God like never before. I am free to love, laugh, and rejoice once more.

SEASON OF RESTORATION

What does it mean "to restore"? There are several definitions for the term, these include "bringing back," "repairing," "renovating," "reinstating or returning to a former or original condition, place, or position."

Why would a person want to restore something or someone? In my estimation, there has to be love involved. There has to be respect and the knowledge that the thing or person to be restored has worth or value. For restoration to take place, there has to be knowledge of the importance of preservation. By this, I mean that when we understand the relevance of a thing or person, we do not place them into a disposable position. We look for ways, means, and opportunities to bring them back to their former glory.

So when do we consider restoration? Obviously, not before there is some form of loss. This loss could be physical, spiritual, financial, or even social, as it relates to God's ordination and intent.

What is the narrative of your life? Have you been buffeted on every side? Has life beaten you down? Have you been feeling less than you know you ought to? Do you feel hopeless, confused, and disoriented today?

You can trust God for restoration! That is why He had me writing this book. Yes, today can be your day of mending. He still regenerates and renews. He still rejuvenates and revives. He is, even as I type, restoring many things to me. He'll restore many things to you as well as you read this book.

Across the expanse of the earth: He is restoring lives, lost hope, courage, health, wealth, families, relationships, opportunities among untold things. He is the *Great Restorer*.

How can I receive restoration? you may ask. My friend, through the pages of the Bible, we see the promises of God. He promises to restore. He promises to return our favours. He promises to bless and do us good, but we must be ready to receive.

The chief restoration blocker is the devil, whose aim is to steal, kill, and destroy. If he is able to persuade you that you have no worth, he has already defeated you. If he can convince you that you are broken and irreparable, he has already won the battle. My friend, Jesus is the restorer or repairer of broken walls. He is the potter who is capable of mending any broken pottery pieces. He is excited to help you return to your former glory.

Former glory is not only indicative of a relapse into bad ways or error (backsliding) but also to the time when a person once had things that he has now lost. In short, former glory indicates that something of beauty or worth has been lost.

It is written in Joel 2:21, "Fear not, O land; be glad and rejoice: for the LORD will do great things." I hereby decree and declare, by virtue of the promises of God, that your life will not regress, but you shall mount up with wings like an eagle. You shall rejoice and be glad, based on what the Lord shall do in your life. It's your season and your time. Mount up in God, the God of your salvation. Arise and be counted worthy of your calling. Walk into the perfect will and purpose of your Lord and Savior. You are blessed and highly favoured, my friend. Arise and praise the Lord, for today, victory awaits you in Jesus's name.

> He raiseth up the poor out of the dust, and lifteth up the beggar from the dunghill, to set them among princes, and to make them inherit the throne of glory: for the pillars of the earth are the LORD'S, and He hath set the world upon them. (1 Samuel 2:8)

Declaration

Today, I choose life over loss. I decree and declare that because my confidence is in God, I will not be defeated. As an eagle, I rise in the newness of life, knowing full well that I shall prevail against every contrary wind!

FREED BY THE POWER OF FORGIVENESS

Has someone ever said something to or about you that *cut* you to the core? Have you ever been wronged to the point where you felt as though you could never possibly speak to him or her again, much less extend forgiveness? Better yet, has someone ever placed you in a position that caused your reputation and character to be questioned and you were as innocent as a lamb? What about someone taking something you held dear and making a great swat at your trust by not repaying or giving it back to you?

Fret not, Joseph went through all the above and more but conquered bitterness and unforgiveness. His story was included in the Bible so that you and I can garner hope and enjoy peace of mind amid adversity. This story brings home the profound reality that in the end, good always prevails over evil, and there is a just recompense for waiting on God and trusting Him wholeheartedly, no matter what trial faces us.

When we read the story today (Genesis 37 and 39), we see the rise, betrayal, fall, and perpetual elevation of a man who overcame life's challenges in a magnanimous way. Do you believe that Joseph knew his story would have made it into the Bible? Do you think that he knew there would be a profound legacy and lesson to be garnered from his life of pains, hurt, and rejection? I think not, beloved!

This guy was supernaturally gifted but humble and innocent, so much so that he was taken for granted. When you are gifted, as long as you remain humble, you will be taken for granted. Jesus had the same experience. Do you remember that? So what in heaven or earth has given you that brilliant idea that you will be exempted from fiery trials? In a discussion with *His* disciples, Jesus asked them, "If they do this to a green tree, what will happen to a dry one?" (Luke 23:31). What fault was found in Jesus? Like a green tree that is in its prime and not fit for burning or to be used as lumber, Jesus was in his early stage when they sought to kill *Him*. Even during His infancy, without any sin or having done no wrong, *His* life was sought. What about you and I today?

So the story of Joseph continues, he was so unique that he saw profound things in his sleep that had deep spiritual connotations and relevance. Not only did he dream, but he was enabled by God to understand and interpret what was shown to him. He didn't know if he should see his gift as a blessing or curse because some of them were mind-boggling and bordered on alarming. In fact, his dreams were what led to him experiencing his siblings' full wrath and, at one point, his father's scoff of disapproval. Jacob (his dad) couldn't accept that the dream of the sun and moon bowing to worship Joseph could be referring to him. He was thoroughly offended and chided him for even daring to share such a dream.

Joseph's dreams led to resentment, and soon he was flung into a pit by his jealous and wicked brothers. They wanted to see the end of him! They desperately needed him to get out of the way, especially when it got to the point of their father making him a coat of many colors. The average person may say that Jacob was, in part, to be blamed for instigation rivalry among his children. I beg to disagree because I know that when you are specially selected by God, you will be marked by favour. The coat signified much because, from all indications, Joseph's life was quite colorful. Even as he rose to become the prime minister, he dealt with people of different nationalities. This is because, during that time, Egypt held world power, and merchants and other people of great significance traversed that region.

The same brothers who put Joseph through hell were the ones he was anointed to preserve. He was their forerunner to Egypt, to activate the power of preservation. Had they not hated him so badly that they placed him in a pit and the same day sold him to Ishmaelite merchants, the Ishmaelite merchants wouldn't have sold him to

Potiphar. Had Potiphar not bought and placed him as head of his affairs, he wouldn't have met his wife whose wantonness led her to desire to have sex with him. Had he not escaped as she tried to lie with him, leaving a piece of his garment in her hand, he would not have gone to the prison. Had he not been sent to prison because of her cruel lies, he wouldn't have met the baker and cupbearer whose dreams he interpreted. Had he been removed from prison before the time, the King Pharaoh may never have learnt of him. Had Pharaoh not learnt of him, he wouldn't have been able to interpret the king's dream, thus being promoted to not head of a household this time but the prime minister of the entire country.

Beloved friend, Joseph should have and could have become bitter by life's darts, but he did not. In fact, because of his steadfast love and dedication to God amid adversity, he found favour at every level of trial.

So what lesson do I want you to take away from our conversation today? I need you to forgive. Forgive those who have hurt you. Forgive those who have repeatedly buffeted you. Forgive, forgive, and forgive some more. Your haters can't stop you, but unforgiveness *will* not only stop you but will cripple your life.

Is forgiveness an easy task? No, I'm going to keep it real, because this book is geared at helping you. I'm not going to sugarcoat anything because that's lying. Deception, jealousy, false accusation, rejection, and hatred hurt, and you know what, they cut deep! If not handled properly, these things can lead to bitterness and even murder, but guess what? How will those things help you? What exactly do you seek in your life? Do you desire peace of mind? Do you desire a close walk with God? *Is* heaven your destination? If so, you have to let things go. You have to feel stabs in your back and still love the stabbers. Guess what, my dear friend? You can't do this by sheer goodness of heart but only by God's grace. By *His* enabling power, you can and will overcome unforgiveness. He says cast every care on *Him*. He says all vengeance is *His*. Commit your ways to *Him* right now, and *He* will help you. *He* will not fail nor forsake you. It is His good pleasure that you be delivered from the yolk of bitterness and unforgiveness. I give you Jesus Christ of Nazareth today, friend. Believe me when I tell you, *He* is the heavy load carrier. He is the burden bearer. Cast all your hurts on *Him*, and *He* will give you relief and sweet rest!

> Forbearing one another, and forgiving one another, if any man have a quarrel against any: even as Christ forgave you, so also do ye. (Colossians 3:13)

Declaration

Today, I choose to walk in the path of forgiveness. As I forgive others, I receive the cleansing relief of forgiveness. I am forgiven and set free. My heart is no longer a captive of hurt. I am no longer bound by the chains of bitterness, anger, malice, and strife because I choose to forgive myself as well as others.

A NEW THING AWAITS

Even as a little girl, I cherished new things especially since they were far in between. Back then, I was never as elated as when I got my *stuff*. This was because I was most times the recipient of things that were handed down from my cousins. I was the youngest girl at home, and being very skinny, I didn't receive things, such as clothes, from my older sister, but for sure, I knew that my cousins would have some things that they had outgrown, and these would be coming to me.

My mother always reminded me to be grateful for everything because some kids were in far worse positions than I was. This did not stop me from shouting with glee when I would be given brand-new things that I knew were all mine. Soon, I began to look forward to Christmas, because most times, I would receive something that no one else had worn or ever owned. As a result of what I anticipated, Christmas then became a very special time of the year for me. Sometimes, when I got a new dress, I would discard an old one or two. This would more often than not get me into trouble, but the new dress or, on rare occasions, dresses were sufficient to ease whatever punishment would be meted for this supposed waste. As I look back on those years, I realize that I was practicing the new thing mentality.

So what old thing holds you captive? Today, I submit to you that these things are meant to be removed from your life. You can be set free from the bondage of your past. You can be loosed from the shackles and pains of yesterday. You have no control over what transpired when you were a child. You may be the survivor of a broken marriage and a wrecked home. The sorrows and shame of yesteryears' woes may be your tale. You may have a colorful yesterday that even now seeks to keep you bound. You may have been used and abused and feel like a broken and discarded doll to this very day of your life. You may feel hopeless, helpless, and trapped in the mire of history, but today I declare that it's your season of breakthrough and liberty. You are not destined to remain a prisoner! Receive the freedom you have long desired. Break free from the bonds of your past. Enjoy the new lease He is giving you on life. Receive *newness*, and soar to the height to which you are destined.

> Therefore if any man be in Christ, he is a
> new creature: old things are passed away; behold
> all things are become new. (2 Corinthians 5:17)

Declaration

I break free from every cage of the past in the mighty name of Jesus. With hind feet, I climb over walls of past pains and shame. By the power of Jesus Christ, the new me is emerging. I am transitioning from glory to glory! Everyone that beholds me shall be astounded by the masterpiece that I have become by the power of God!

THE REVIVED REMNANT

A remnant is the small remaining portion of a thing or a group of people. Despite its size, a remnant is relevant as it portrays or is a reflection of what the whole might or could have been.

As revealed in the scriptures, from Genesis to Revelation, the children of Israel are the remnant of God. They were not chosen because of their size, as they were the fewest in number, of all the nations, nor were they selected based on righteousness, for there was none that was righteous. They were selected under the covenant-keeping mandate of God. Once God promises to bless a nation, *He* blesses it, and when He plans to curse it, that is exactly what *He* does. Having made a covenant with Abraham, *He* would never break it. Notwithstanding *His* mercy, the nation of Israel suffered much pain and sorrow because they continuously went against the will of God, thus provoking *His* wrath.

They were so rebellious and unrepentant that many times the Lord God caused their enemies to rise against and defeat them. It wasn't His will to bring them pain, but as a result of their waywardness, they would manage to move away from Him, their edge of protection. This moving away always made them a snare to their enemies. Despite their wantonness, by virtue of his loving-kindness, whenever they cried to *Him*, God would always extend mercy and send *His* word to heal them. He would prove Himself as their deliverer, thus rescuing them from every undesirable situation, in which they found themselves.

Notwithstanding their constant backsliding, the children of Israel knew that life, without God at the center was truly no life at all. This was what drove them to repentance each time. They saw their afflictions and understood the root cause each time. They also knew that the plans of God toward them were for good and not evil. Many times, the children of Israel wept and travailed as they sought to get to a place of revival and restitution. One such powerful and heartrending message is seen in Psalm 137: "*By the rivers of Babylon, there we sat down, yea, we wept, when we remembered Zion.*"

My friend, as it was in the beginning, so it is now: We continue to experience pain and distress as a result of our stubbornness. God, however, who is plenteous in grace, continues to make a way for us to escape. His desire is for us to form a relationship with *Him* so *He* can fight on our behalf, thus helping us to overcome sin. *He* knows our common enemy. He knows our frailty. He knows satan only comes to steal, kill, and destroy. Since God's desire is for us to be a part of the remnant generation, *He* continues to gather us as a hen gathers her chicks.

The main lesson we need to learn from Israel's history is that a life severed from God is a worthless one. We also need to use them as an example of what God does or allows when we depart from a relationship with *Him*. As we reflect on the words of our Lord and Savior, we need to understand that constant connection is preferred to revival.

As the writer Hosea reminds us, we must return unto the *Lord*: for *He* hath torn, and *He* will heal us; *He* hath smitten, and *He* will bind us up. *No* matter what the circumstances of our lives are, we have hope in *His* love. Despite our shortcomings and failures, we can rest assured that because mercy and truth met at the *cross*, there was a marriage of the earth and sky. Through this merge, there was reversed captivity, the forgiveness and burial of sin, the dispelling of dark clouds of separation, and the speaking of peace and goodwill to all men.

David captures it best when he said, "As the hart pants after the water brook so my soul longs for you! May we desire more of God every day." May we hunger and thirst after righteousness. My beloved friends, may we seek to remain in the secret place of the most high. In *His* presence, there is fullness of joy, and at *His* right hand, are pleasures for ever more.

Wilt thou not revive us again: that thy people may rejoice in thee? (Psalm 85:6)

Declaration

I am set apart for the glory of God. I am a joint heir with *Jesus* and a part of the kingdom of life! I am His, and He is mine! Glory be to God Most High!

TRUST DIVINE PROVIDENCE

To fully understand the divine providence of God, my friend, you must understand *His* nature. Jehovah God, the Abba of the redeemed and the one that created all living things, is faithful. He is not a man that *He* should lie; neither is *He* the son of man that *He* should repent. If *He* promises it, *He* will do it. When *He* said *He* would be with us always, that's what *He* meant. He is not slack concerning *His* promises. *He* is the Promise Keeper and Way Maker. *He* is the Light of the world.

He is willing and able to divinely provide for those who hope in Him and have made him their confidence. None that trusts in *Him* shall ever be ashamed. God is so very caring that whatever *He* must, *He* will do to ensure that the needs of His creations are met.

My friend, another thing that we must remember is that God, as Creator, has all we need. He is the One who created heaven and earth. He is rich in houses and lands. He holds the wealth of the world in *His* hand. He has a hallmark of trustworthiness as *He* says, "I am the way, the truth, and the life." In light of these facts, we must be very deliberate in ensuring that we trust Him. Nothing is impossible for *Him* to do except to lie. This is why now and then, *He* will and, therefore, bid *His* servants hide toward the sunrise, but in these periods of enforced seclusion, He makes Himself responsible for their supplies. The Prophet Elijah is a prime example.

> So he went and did according unto the word of the LORD: for he went and dwelt by the brook Cherith that *is* before Jordan. And the

ravens brought him bread and flesh in the morning, and bread and flesh in the evening; and he
drank of the brook. (1 Kings 17:5–6)

Declaration

The Lord is my keeper and my provider. I trust Him for my daily
sustenance. All of my help cometh from the God of my *salvation*.

THE BECOMING SEASON

Dear friend, where are you now? What do you desire to see happening in your life? Do you possess a strong desire to rise above limitations? Are you ready to rise above every stagnant situation that may be holding you back? Do you wish to escape the pit of complacency and needless delays that life has been throwing your way? Do you wish to mount up with wings like an eagle? You must put to silence the voice that is trying to hold you back mentally, telling you that you cannot make it? Your past doesn't have to intercept your present? Allow God to free you from every shackles of your past! Look unto Jesus, the Christ—*the All-Sufficient One*! *He* is the *I Am* that I Am and the never-failing One.

This God gives grace and capability to all those who dare to believe in and trust *Him* wholeheartedly. He never fails nor forsakes them that look to *Him* for help. When we truly meet and develop a relationship with Him, we discover that *He* can and will become our cornerstone. Life with Christ causes us to recognize our frailties and limitations but allows us to know what we can become through Him. It is then that we discover how much more we can get done through *His* grace than by our human strength and effort.

It would surprise you to understand how much you can accomplish and truly *achieve* when you allow God to become your everlasting portion. As *He* becomes whatever you desire *Him* to be, you become whatever *He* desires you to be, since your relationship now becomes a reciprocal one. The simple truth is that when *He* becomes your *I Am* that *I Am*, you automatically receive heavenly benefits and reinforcement, which cause you to become undefeated and indomi-

73

table. You become a force to be reckoned with. As you throw yourself on *Him* with reckless abandon, *He* becomes your battering ram, and you become an enigma to your enemies.

When you receive *Him* into your heart and walk with *Him* in truth and sincerity, you become a shareholder of heaven. You are now a joint heir and brother of Jesus who gives you power over all powers of the enemy!

It is doubtful that anyone made such a startling discovery as did David when he said and I quote, "*I* will both lay me down in peace, and sleep: for thou, LORD, only makest me dwell in safety." If you are desirous of confident dependence and peace of mind, you need not look further than David's Psalms. While many more Bible characters saw God's power and trusted *Him* fully, there is something about David. Most of his Psalms highlighted and repeatedly mentioned the reliability of God.

Beloved friend, trust *Him* absolutely, not just today but for all ages! Rest assured that God holds a reputation of infallibility and consistency. He is dependable and reliable. He sticks closer than a brother. He will never fail or forsake you. He will be with you to the end of time and throughout eternity. What hope, consolation, and peace divine?

> But as many as received him, to them gave
> He power to become the sons of God, even to
> them that believe on his name. (John 1:12)

Declaration

I am a recipient of the power of God Almighty. Every day, in every way, I am becoming better and better because of the power of God that rests upon me!

UNLEASH THE HIGHER ORDER THINKING

The *higher-order thinking* is what helps us to understand the power of the spoken word. Do you know how to conquer your words? First, you must be able to conquer your thoughts. "Why is this?" you ask. Your thoughts give birth to your words, and your words become your action or reality.

Don't leave a word idle thought in your mind. If you do so, it will gradually emerge. Declare a word over your thought, which will paralyze it thus, preventing it from manifesting.

So, friend, here's how it works, if you know how to control your thoughts, you know the words to speak and those to leave unspoken. With the higher-order thinking syndrome, however, you take things a bit further. Instead of allowing idle, impure, belittling, angry, or any negative thoughts to swirl around in your mind and remain unspoken, which will be gradually spoken anyway, speak a word over that thought. When this is done, that first thought becomes captivated or paralyzed or simply deactivated. So what happens is that it dies even before being birthed. This aborted thought prevents the birthing of a word that could be used to your detriment.

Here's an example, a mutual friend—of my husband and I—once said, in a conversation, that he's a law-abiding citizen. To prove this, he knew he was above being penalized for anything except in the event of an accident. So confident was he, of his moral standing, that he indicated that he could only be imprisoned one way. This was if he should accidentally kill someone while driving. Needless to say, about a week later, he was behind bars for road fatality. What am I saying? Conquer your words by the higher-order thinking syndrome, and they won't become your reality. My husband told our friend to destroy that word, with a higher word, but clearly, he lacked the wisdom to do so.

So, friend, here's what the *Word of God* says, "As a man thinks, so is he." What is this saying? A man's thoughts become his words. This happens when his thoughts take on flesh and manifest themselves in words, then deeds. Sure enough, what he keeps saying is who he is daily becoming.

Here's what the *Word of God* also says, "Faith is the substance of things hoped for and the evidence of things not seen." Likewise, the *Word of God* says, "Work without faith is dead."

Do you want to understand this practically? It all goes back to your thoughts and words. When you understand the power of the tongue, you recognize that if you think it, you can activate it by speaking it, and it's going to become your reality. So, for example, if you feel sick, go to the doctor and are declared sick, but reject sickness by first your thought, then your word; you will be well again.

This is a simple truth: God wishes above all things that our bodies prosper and be in good health, even as our souls prosper. That being said, we understand that God wants us to be healthy. He designed us to be well. Sicknesses and diseases came upon the earth as a result of the fall of man through sin. So here's how you can be healed. First, believe the written word of God. Think about that word; speak that word over the sickness declaration made by you, friends, family, and even your doctor. This is when the "higher order thinking" syndrome becomes an active antioxidant. Faith now begins to be activated, and guess what? Over time, as you keep speaking that word, it begins to counteract and flush your body, thus, becoming your truth. What was a stronghold of sickness and infirmity now becomes a plane of health. Where the words of the doctor's verdict, alongside your conviction and that of others were, these are replaced. As you intensify speaking health over yourself or situation, the rule of engagement, which creates balance, causes you to become proactive. Now you not only declare healing, but you get off your bed, begin to eat, exercise, go for short and gradually long walks (breathing in

God's fresh air), begin to appreciate God and life on a greater level, and soon and very soon, guess what? Faith with work, activate your healing. The person who was sick is now made whole.

So, friend, you aren't lying when you're faced with any challenge in life and you declare the opposite of what you're facing. What's happening is that you are speaking and acting under the influence of the higher-order thinking syndrome of *God*, your *Creator*. That's what the songwriter wanted you and I to understand when he penned the words of the song "Give Thanks from a Grateful Heart." As you declare the words "I am strong" when you feel weak and "I am rich" when you don't even have a penny in your purse or wallet, they become your reality. You are no longer looking at your current situation but by faith acknowledging what's about to happen. Sooner than later, your word becomes your reality. Now, you understand that "As a man thinks, so is he." You cannot rise higher than your thoughts, neither can you sink lower than they are.

God bless you real good as you watch your thoughts and actively maintain a healthy atmosphere and lifestyle.

> For though we live in the world, we do not wage war as the world does. The weapons we fight with are not the weapons of the world. On the contrary, they have divine power to demolish strongholds. We demolish arguments and every pretension that sets itself up against the knowledge of God, and we take captive every thought to make it obedient to Christ. (2 Corinthians 10:3–5)

Declaration

I take authority over my thoughts and imagination. I exercise power over every high thing in my mind. I bring them under the captivity of the Holy Ghost, in Jesus's name. My tongue is that of an anointed speaker!

SEASON OF APPRECIATION

Hey, friend, how is your day going? What kind of season are you experiencing in your neck of the woods?

There is such bliss to be experienced as we walk outdoors, wouldn't you say? As for me, the wonder of nature always heightens my awareness of the creative power of our *Creator*. I am sure that you will agree with me that once you are paying attention, you get an encounter with the thoughtfulness and amazing artistry of God. There is something simply fascinating for me when I look at the trees, when I stop to look at a chipmunk scurrying up the branches of a tree, and even when I hear a dog barking. My heart never ceases to overflow with gratitude when I think of the greatness of our heavenly Father.

So here's my question, friend, have you ever stopped to consider how tiny squirrels are and how unbothered they seem as they scurry to gather their supplies? What of tons of other wild animals that have no owner? Do you know that God is their Owner and Master? Have you ever considered that God provides for them too? When have you last stopped to pay attention to whatever natural habitats surround you? If God takes care of nature, won't He take care of you too?

At times, when I look at the formation of birds in the sky, I smile and say, "Oh my God, how great thou art!" Once, I stopped to watch a flight of pigeons circle a certain area of the sky a few times and then landed on the ground. It was the most amazing sight that I beheld. For me, that was a reflection of unison, at the highest level. They syncopated so well that my worry proved to be in vain. I should have known that their landing would be smooth, if their flight was anything by which to judge them. Those birds landed in such an incredible way that I almost started clapping. I realize quickly, however, that if I did, I would have scared them away. Boy, were they many? I think there might have been more than two dozen of them, and they landed gracefully, out of each other's path. There was such unison and cohesiveness that I was shocked.

All of God's creation reminds us of His love. Friend, enjoy your natural surrounding, and when you have nothing else for which to be grateful, give thanks if you can see, smell, taste, feel, and hear. God considered well the things He wanted you to enjoy before He gave you your senses.

So today, while I walked, though it was and is still cold (I'm indoors again) with snow lying on the ground, I turned my face heavenward, and as the wind gently kissed my cheek, I thought, *How beautiful it is to be alive.* It's an amazing feeling to walk and enjoy nature. If you want to come alive, you might want to take a little walk. Get away from the humdrum and enjoy the wind, enjoy the breeze. Yes, sometimes all you need is a walk in the rain. Listen, my friend, I love nature, so I am not being silly here. I simply want you to enjoy the here and now. Enjoy what's available.

So many are bedridden today. So many have never seen the light of day. So many would do anything to enjoy a gentle breeze again. My friend, enjoy the simple things of life, and the greater ones will gradually find you. When they do, you'll smile in much appreciation. If life gets too much, take a walk, laugh aloud, do a little skip, and say, "Thank you, Lord." This too shall pass. Have a blessed day.

The heavens declare the glory of God; and
the firmament sheweth his handywork. Day unto
day uttereth speech, and night unto night sheweth
knowledge. There is no speech nor language,
where their voice is not heard. (Psalm 19:1–4)

Declaration

All day, every day, I embrace an attitude of gratitude. I will always strive to find a reason for which I should rejoice.

STAND FAST, IT'S NOT OVER UNTIL IT'S OVER

Hey, friend, I understand that some days seem stagnant and disheartening. Some days your cross seems heavy to bear. Indeed on some days, there is more pain than pleasure and you wonder, "*Why am I here?*" Do you think I don't know that feeling? Wow! So why on God's green earth would I be speaking to you like this? I have been there (smiling). There were days when tears ran silently and unchecked down my cheeks, even as I encouraged someone on the phone. I would be telling them that everything would be okay when I wasn't *feeling* okay myself. Isn't that funny? Was I lying? No, I kept believing that God was with me and would see me through amidst all odds, which He always did by the way.

Friend, two of the scriptures that I found the hardest to understand and appreciate during those early birthing periods of pain were *1 Corinthians 15:36 and John 12:24*. I call those early birthing pains because God was processing me for a new life, and it was very painful at times. I had no idea I was a planted seed.

The reason why I struggled with those scriptures was because I lacked the understanding of the process. I failed to recognize that before a tree came into existence, a seed was planted. It died to itself, meaning that it ceased to be a seed so that the plant would live. Once planted, it no longer found its identity in that of its old self, a seed. In that way, it died; it ceased to exist as its original self. It now became something far different and lived a new kind of life.

My friend, from the *potential* of life that is contained within the seed comes a new life capable of producing fruit. Where a seed cannot produce fruit, its plant form can. It can't do this on its own though; it needs to be planted, nurtured, and nourished.

You are a seed of greatness. You must die to self, people's opinion, sensitivity, and many more things for you to manifest.

Okay, so it took me a long time, perhaps too long, to die, but I'm glad I did because that is why you are reading this book today. You see, friend, many people forget that there are different types of death. Many people fail to understand that to grow, they must lose themselves and find their true identity in their Maker. Sometimes, while on the ground, they depended on the wrong persons or sources for nourishment, and that's why they almost got wasted.

Here's another thing that happens in the transition process, sometimes after the seed becomes a tree, the top of the tree dies. Oh boy, does trouble ever ceases? (Laughing.) There are so many things that happen during the birthing and the growing season of our lives, but that is how we unlearn to learn and become who we ought to be.

So here's a bit that you might not know about a tree: It tries to maintain a balance between the top and the underground system since there's a constant flow both ways. If the tree loses roots, it's also going to lose something aboveground. It is experiencing root stress! "Wonder of wonders," you say. "Do tree roots experience stress too?" Sure they do! This tree root stress is known as root girdling—when the roots coil around the base and constrict the flow of sap. This can happen when trees are grown in containers, and the problem is exacerbated when they are brought home from the nursery and planted too deep.

Another factor that can lead to the death of the top part of a tree is a lack of adequate water. "Most of our watering is often too little." So here is the shocker, you and I must be well watered for us to stay alive in adversity. Sure, it's okay for the seed to die, but when a tree is the result, why should the tree die at least before its time? We know, this top dying of a tree is abnormal because it's either full death or no death. We cannot be half dead.

The final aspect of tree growth molestation that I want to look at is insects! Bark beetles, such as emerald ash borers and bronze birch borers, are a less common cause of the decline of the top of your tree, and most commonly affect very young or old trees.

Yes, insects cause trouble for many trees and so are some circumstances in lives. They are like insects. They plague us! They eat away at our bodies, minds, and will. They are the little foxes that spoil the vine. Sometimes, these insects are within. They are the little bad habits we entertain. The belittling thoughts we have about ourselves. The doubts, the fears, and yes, the insecurities, which gnaws at our inner man, telling us that we cannot accomplish big things. Those demonic whisperings of our past failures and mistakes! At other times, these insects are in the form of negative people and outer sources and factors. People who are willing to lie on, use, and abuse us! People who will attempt to ridicule, ostracize, and persecute us.

That's right, they must die today. If I was able to write this book, what can't you do? I was told I would amount to nothing. I was told I wasn't going to make it. Do you know how much I fought against those utterances? Do you know what I discovered about myself? I enjoy challenges. Oh yes, those little foxes tested me, and I was not going to fail. I told them, if you are ready, let the fight begin. They all died en route because I won them. I put an end to their mischief, and so can you, my friend.

I need you to know that if you are a believer, the hand of the Lord is upon you! If you are not a believer, He desires a relationship with you. He knows your name! He remembers you! He knows what is currently happening in your life. He sees your pains, and He understands your brokenness. His greatest desire is to lead you into your divine destiny so you can accomplish His perfect plan. Yes, friend, His desire is for you to fulfill the numbers of your days.

Though you may be going through a season of drought, you don't have to die and shouldn't die once you are reading this book. He wants to lead you beside still water. Don't resist Him; He only desires to breathe life into your circumstances. He is about to make all things beautiful for you. Don't give up on God because He hasn't and won't give up on you. Yes! It looks dead—in fact, *it is dead*! It even stinks, but at the moment you least expect it, God will show up.

He will put flesh on the skeletal area of your life because He loves you with everlasting love.

You shall testify! You shall rise above this! Hello, are you hearing me? Come on, child of God, hallelujah, this too shall pass. It's your season of change. Come on now, that which the cankerworms and caterpillars have eaten is about to be restored. You shall recover! You shall recover! You shall recover! You shall recover! You shall recover! You shall recover! You shall recover! You shall recover it all!

> And he said unto me, Son of man, can these bones live? And I answered, O LORD GOD, thou knowest. Again he said unto me, Prophesy upon these bones, and say unto them, O ye dry bones, hear the word of the LORD. Thus saith the LORD God unto these bones; Behold, I will cause breath to enter into you, and ye shall live: And I will lay sinews upon you, and will bring up flesh upon you, and cover you with skin, and put breath in you, and ye shall live; and ye shall know that I am the LORD. (Ezekiel 37:1, 3–6)

Declaration

My kiros moment is now! It's my season...I stand in faith! Today I rise above every limitations! I stand my ground and win every battle that faces me in the mighty name of Jesus Christ of Nazareth!

IT'S THE WINNOWING SEASON,
WHAT'S YOUR POSITION?

Well, hello there, friend, it's such a pleasure to stop by to share this thought with you today. Have you ever heard the word *winnowing* before? When that word came to me, I was a little taken aback. As far as I can recall, it wasn't one of the most frequently used ones in my schema. As a result, I had no idea why I would include it here. Nonetheless, since the Master downloaded it, I figured, why not? If He says it's your winnowing season, that's what it is. Well, you are indeed on point: If God gives a word, He will make provision for greater and deeper revelation, hence, the discussion at hand.

While there are various aspects to winnowing, the one I wish to concentrate on is *wind winnowing*. This is an agricultural method developed by ancient cultures for separating grains from straws. It was also a strategy used to remove pests from stored grains. Winnowing usually followed threshing in grain preparation. In its simplest form, wind winnowing involved throwing the mixture into the air so that the wind blew away the chaff while the grains fell for recovery. This technique included using a winnowing fan (a shaped basket shaken to raise the chaff) or the usage of a tool (a winnowing fork or shovel) on a pile of harvested grain.

As I looked more deeply into the word, winnowing, my friend, "separation" leaped at me. Just the same way that farmers use winnowing as an extrication method, so it is that God uses his own strategy for sorting out and separating his people.

Throughout the scriptures, we see that there are in fact two different types or kinds of people. One set always chooses good and the other evil. The reason behind this is because there are two forces that are activated by two different spirits. God is the ruler and instigator of all that is good and holy while satan, his archenemy, is the instigator of all that is evil and unholy. As the ages roll by, we see greater manifestations and operations of the evil one. This is not to say that evil exceeds good; however, evil is like oil on water: It swims on top and gives the impression that it is greater or stronger than its counterpart—good, which far outweighs it all the time. This of course, my friend, is because the wicked one—satan—is a deceiver and the father of all lies. That is, all lies emanate from him. As a result, he always exaggerates and blows things out of proportion.

I know you are getting the picture quite clearly, my friend. *Yes,* there is a need for severance because there is no middle ground in the kingdom of God or the kingdom of darkness. We are either fully on one side or the other. Do you remember that I told you the devil or satan is a liar? Well, he is also a trickster. It is not surprising therefore that he often encourages people, even professed believers, to daub into a little wrongdoing here or there under the guise that their god will understand and will not hold it against them. Of course, friend, once they (believers) indulge in such folly, that old dragon scoffs and laughs at them. The reason why he does these despicable things is because he knows that once more, one of his lies worked.

Hello, friend, we can never be on both sides of the fence, and that is what a lot of people fail to recognize. We are either a soldier in Jesus' army or we are a part of satan's army. God deals with order while satan enjoys and encourages confusion.

Several scriptures clearly point to the fact that there is the need for coming out from "among them," that is, the things, lifestyles, and companionship that God despises. We are also admonished to know where we stand because there is great recompense for those on God's side and equal punishment for those on the side of the evil one.

Even as I write today, the wind of change is blowing briskly across the land. We are in perilous times. These are the last days, and as such, the war in the spirit realm is intensifying. There is an urgent separation that is happening in various ways and phases. You see, friend, as I said before, there is no middle ground when it comes to the spirit realm. God is, therefore, looking for true soldiers, soldiers that will be loyal to him and his kingdom agenda.

He is pruning many through fiery trials because fire is known to destroy and is also a good source of separation and qualification. As a goldsmith places gold into the fire, we see that all impurities die while the gold comes alive. Its true beauty is revealed and released in the kilning process. The grueling process of fire is indeed a winnowing technique. When the wind doesn't work, the fire does. Indeed, as we draw closer to the end of this age—the last days—there is a line of demarcation drawn.

My dear friend, if you are unsure where you stand in this season, now is an excellent time to figure it out. My humble recommendation is that you join Jesus's army. Say yes to him today because there is an allotted time given to you and me. Of course, none of us know the length of our days. Many persons would have made better decisions if they knew their time and hour of departing this life.

I assure you most boldly that you have an assigned time to kiss this world goodbye. In case you are wondering how to navigate your way unto the Lord's side, here are a few simple steps:

1. Believe and have faith: Hebrews 11:6, Mark 16:16.
2. Confess your sins and repent: 1 John 1:9, Acts 2:38.
3. Confess him as Lord and Savior: Matthew 10:32.
4. Be baptized in his name: Mark 16:16, Acts 2:38.
5. Live a Godly life, which is the new birth: 2 Peter 3:11, Ephesians 4:1, Colossians 1:10.

If you were a part of Jesus's army and for one reason or another deserted it, now is a good time to return. He is forever married to the backsliders! He is forever asking them to come home!

> Then Moses stood in the gate of the camp, and said, Who is on the LORD'S side? let him come unto me. And all the sons of Levi gathered themselves together unto him. (Exodus 32:26)

Declaration

I know who I am and whose I am. Today I choose life over pleasure. Today, I stand on the Solid Rock Jesus Christ. I am a soldier in the Lord's army!

RELEASED TO BE REFRESHED

A heat wave surging across a place will cause many people to seek a cool and refreshing drink. For many, lemonade is one of the best options. Why is this? Because it stimulates salivation.

When someone becomes dehydrated on a hot day, his body's need for liquid manifests as a dry mouth. When something that has a sour taste is placed into the mouth, it causes salivation. This kind of taste encourages salivation more than any other taste. On the other hand, when acidic liquids are placed into the mouth, hydration occurs, even after the lemonade or vinegar water is finished.

David himself knew thirst but of a different kind. No amount of kingly riches, accolades, fame, or popularity could quench this thirst. He desired a deep and long-lasting relationship with his God—the very Maker of heaven and earth. This desire was such that it could neither be quenched by man or beast. In his quest, he found Him whom His soul loved, and that was all the satisfaction needed.

Are you tired, weary, and worn? Are you heavy laden with a load of care? Would you like to meet God by the river of His word today? Will you allow prayer to wash and refresh your heart? You, who are thirsty for healing and happiness, will you say yes to the Life Giver—Jesus Christ? He wants to quench your soul's thirst! He wants to make wrongs right. God wants to do for you more than you can imagine or ask!

Today can be the start of a brand-new season in your life, friend! Listen to your inner man and do it. Say "yes" and allow God to take full control and give you a new lease on life. He will satisfy you in ways you didn't even imagine He could. He will rearrange your life and syncopate you with your divine destiny! Oh yes, beloved, He will bring you a deep-settled peace and take you to new and unknown heights. Lean upon Jesus, and walk confidently and boldly into this season. Fear not, He will guide you to the end.

> As the hart panteth after the water brooks,
> so panteth my soul after thee, O God. My soul
> thirsteth for God, for the living God: when shall
> I come and appear before God? (Psalm 42:1)

Declaration

Today I choose to embrace the new lease I've received on life. I allow myself to let go and let God! I surrender my life to His total control. Today, I acknowledge and embrace Him as my Sovereign Lord: the only One who can fulfill all the longings and desires of my heart.

THERE IS A RIVER

A river is a sure sign of life. It is an indication of the possibility of growth, replenishment, and prosperity.

A river has different meanings and relevance to different people and things. To the fisherman, it's a means of livelihood. To the nature lover, it is another of the wonders of God's artistry and grandeur, but to the habitats of the water, it is life. Without this body of water, they cease to exist.

So who are you? What do you possess? There is a river within you. There is a well of possibilities. Deep within you lies a champion. You are a reservoir of life-changing potential. You are meant to shift the very trajectory of nations and your generation.

Tap into your inner beauty. Activate the life-giving channel within you. Rise to the occasion today because you possess much more than you even know. Oh yes, there is a river of wealth within you. There is a fountain of inner strength. Be the best version of yourself because you were made in the image and likeness of your Lord and Savior. You are meant to shine! Arise and begin to irrigate the dry and parched land around you called life

> There is a river, the streams whereof shall make glad the city of God, the holy place of the tabernacles of the most High. (Psalm 46:4)

Declaration

I am a reservoir of wealthy thoughts, ideas, and potentialities. I am compacted with life-changing possibilities to influence the trajectory of my generation and those to come. I will replenish the lives of many.

SEASON OF HEALING

Are you feeling ill, cumbered, frustrated, fatigued, and bound though you have no idea what is the ailment? Is everything seemingly going wrong in your life during this season although everyone is trying to convince you otherwise? At what point did these occurrences begin? Perhaps it was after a significant breakthrough that you experienced or after a traumatic encounter. During this time, you may have consulted with friends and family members. You may have tried the doctor's prescription. You might have consulted with counselors, therapists, soothsayers, and palm readers. You might have resorted to yoga or other kinds of meditation, but still, the situation hasn't changed: In fact, it may have taken a turn for the worse. Despite the best advice of everyone, things stubbornly refuse to change. You might be carrying this weight for a long time, and though you smile, deep down, you know everything is falling apart.

Perhaps you are now at the breaking point where you are wondering what is next. Is there anyone who can help me? Even as you read right now, you may be at the precipice of disaster. The point where you are filled with despair, wondering, "Will I rise again? Will I be well again?"

Well, you are not alone. Illness, depression, and oppression, contrary to what many think or say, are not just physical but also reflect what first happens in the spirit realm. Yes, there are two realms, the physical and the spiritual. We are sure that we are in the physical realm, but did you know that there are illegal entities that navigate both realms? Yes, though human beings are confined to one realm physically, while some spirits occupy both realms. They travel from the spiritual realm to the earth realm through what we call vortexes. They have good or bad power and can cause harm to human bodies and souls. We are often not aware that some sicknesses, oppression, stagnation, and other such maladies are demonic. The good thing, however, friend, is that no matter what your trouble is, you can receive healing and deliverance. The Balm in Gilead is well able. He can do exceedingly, abundantly above all that you can even think or ask.

In the Bible, we are told of a woman who had a blood disease for twelve years. That was a long time to be sick, wouldn't you agree? Well, that was her situation, and to further complicate things, she had spent all she had, trying to procure healing! She tried every form of physicians, yet nothing worked for her. The truth, friend, is that everything was working against her. As if that was not enough, she was now a pauper, a recluse, and a rejected person. She was scorned by all who knew her.

She was tormented day and night and having nothing left by which to attain her healing; she must have accepted the reality that her case was a hopeless one. Well, all of that changed the day Jesus showed up on her street. You see, friend, Jesus is the ultimate change in a person's life. He can never show up and things remain the same.

The day He arrived in town, the lady did the most dreadful thing that anyone ever dared to do! She, who was unwell, considered filthy and unclean, dared to touch Him! What remarkable faith: This woman supposed in her heart that if she touched Him, something would happen. Yes, she dared to believe, against all odds, that if she could only touch Him, she would be made whole. She did not dare believe that He would touch her; she knew that she had a need, and once she touched His hem, she would be made whole.

Several things happened, leading up to her coming into contact with Jesus. First, she overcame her fear and doubts and accepted that He was the only one who could help her. She decided that whatever happened, she was going to touch Him. Secondly, she was prepared to push against the crowd to get to where she needed to be. She decided that if Jesus was not coming to her, she was going to Him.

Thirdly, she challenged the throng and made the contact, which she believed would change her life forever. Finally, she overcame the fear of touching Jesus because she believed this was her only opportunity to be healed of her infirmity. The moment she lost consciousness of the factors that were hindrances and boulders was the moment that her life changed!

What are your plans today? What ailment do you suffer? Are you willing to touch Jesus? Will you give Him a chance to heal your emotion, body, and spirit? Will you give Jesus your tears so He can turn them into triumph? He is well able to heal, restore, and renew. Give Him full access. Give Him a chance, and you will be glad you did.

> And a certain woman, which had an issue of blood twelve years and had suffered many things of many physicians, and had spent all that she had, and was nothing bettered, but rather grew worse, when she had heard of Jesus, came in the press behind, and touched his garment. For she said, If I may touch but his clothes, I shall be whole. (Mark 5:25–28)

Declaration

Today, I ride on the wind of change. I rise above every limitation, sicknesses, and diseases. Today I triumph by the power of Jesus, which supersedes all power given on earth.

IT'S YOUR JUBILEE

The *Jubilee* (Hebrew: יובל yōḇel; Yiddish: yoyvl) is the year at the end of seven cycles of shmita (Sabbatical years). It deals mainly with land, property, and property rights—hence its name ("Year of Release"). It is a time when the Jews celebrate, by freedom received as slaves, the forgiveness of debt and the particular and obvious manifestation of God's grace and mercies.

In the olden days, the happiest persons during the Jubilee were the slaves and underprivileged people. These were the ones who were always made to feel as though their value to success was irrelevant.

During this special celebration, slaves were granted freedom, and the less fortunate ones had certain privileges granted to them. It was not an everyday occurrence, so everyone made the most of it, knowing it would not return before the next seven years.

Can you imagine gaining freedom after several years of bondage and servitude to a master that you probably did not like in the first place? What an elation and joy unspeakable? What relief freedom gives, right? During Jubilee, those in oblivion and obscurity became recipients of a most fantastic gift, the freedom to choose a new home and family.

Similar to the Israelites who celebrate this occasion, you too can have your season of *jubilee*. Every sin was covered by the blood of Jesus, and so freedom can be attained in your bloodline, business, body, and spirit. It is the Father's good pleasure that you experience restoration and renewal. He wants you to come alive through the blood of Jesus Christ.

Whom the Son sets free is free indeed. Today, if you have made Jesus your choice, you have all right to celebrate. If you have already surrendered to him, rest assured that you have rights to heaven and are currently sitting in heavenly places with Christ your *King*.

But wait, in case you have not yet laid claim to the blood of Jesus or surrendered your life to Him, now is a good time to do it, so you too can celebrate! Today can be the acceptable season of your life. It can be the start of your year of *jubilee*. Jesus wants to make your life glorious. He wants to make you an unmovable oak tree. When Jesus went to the cross, it was to redeem all humanity: Whosoever will can have eternal life. Please understand, friend, that God wants to show forth His praise in your life. It's your chain-breaking season. It's your yoke-breaking season. It is time to make hay while the sun shines, my friend. Make today count. Rise and be counted worthy. It's your season of *jubilee*.

> The Spirit of the Lord God is upon me, because the Lord has anointed me to bring good news to the poor; he has sent me to bind up the brokenhearted, to proclaim liberty to the captives, and the opening of the prison to those who are bound; to proclaim the year of the Lord's favor, and the day of vengeance of our God; to comfort all who mourn; to grant to those who mourn in Zion—to give them a beautiful headdress instead of ashes, the oil of gladness instead of mourning, the garment of praise instead of a faint spirit; that they may be called oaks of righteousness, the planting of the Lord, that he may be glorified. They shall build up the ancient ruins; they shall raise up the former devastations; they shall repair the ruined cities, the devastations of many generations. Strangers shall stand and tend your flocks; foreigners shall be your plowmen and vinedressers. (Isaiah 61:1–11)

Declaration

Today I accept the freedom that Jesus Christ gives. It is my year of *jubilee* and my season for freedom. I walk over high places of limitation and bondage in the exalted name of Jesus.

SEASON OF DANCING

Have you ever stopped to contemplate the seasons? Most places, except for those in the tropics, experience four of them—spring, summer, autumn, and winter. All these occur over a period. Have you noticed that none of them ever last forever? As long, lovely, warm, windy, damp, and dreary as any of them may be, none lasts forever.

Similarly to the seasons, we all have experiences that last for various periods of our lives. Some of them are long and dreary and seem as though they will never end. These are seasons during which we feel as though we will not make it. During these times, we wonder where is the sun? We even ask, where is God?

Be encouraged and know that your season of dancing has arrived! God who has seen your tears is turning things around for you. He promised never to leave you alone, and for sure, He is blessing you abundantly. Yes, for sure, things are not yet where you want them, but they still aren't where they were before. The fact that you are holding this book, friend, is an indication that your dancing season has arrived. It's your season of recovery and regain. You are more blessed than you could ever imagine. Rejoice and be glad in God. He has not forsaken you. He was simply processing you. He loves you with an everlasting love. It's your season for dancing. Rejoice and be exceedingly glad.

> Thou hast turned for me my mourning into dancing: thou hast put off my sackcloth, and girded me with gladness. (Psalm 30:11)

Declaration

My days begin and end with rejoicing and thanksgiving. I surround myself with happy and joyful thoughts. I embrace my season of victory and freedom knowing that God is for me and will never leave or forsake me.

A RAY OF HOPE

The Lord gives strength to those who are weak and ready to rely on Him. He is a balm to the weary and a tower of strength to the feeble.

A prime example of this truth is found in the book of Judges chapter 6. Here we read about a man called Gideon. When we are introduced to him, Gideon is hiding and threshing wheat in a winepress. Did you hear that? A winepress. Whoever does that?

The reason for him hiding was due to the attacks of the enemies on his nation Israel. During this period, most Israelites were in hiding, probably starving as their enemies invaded the land and harvested their crops.

The greeting extended to Gideon by the angel was, "The LORD *is* with thee, thou mighty man of valor." This greeting was considered humorous because Gideon was hiding from the enemy at the time of this salutation. He responded that he came from a low-income family and was not a hero.

Later on, we see how Gideon led his nation to victory through obedience to and reliance on God.

If life seems to be working against you and all hope is gone, this is an excellent time to make a bargain with God. This is the right time to seek Him with your whole heart. Your weakness is a promising avenue for you to prove His strength and might.

Many of my profound God experiences came during the worst and most down and out moments in my life. Several believers testify that the power of God was manifested at a time when they were at *rock bottom* or as is often said, "When their backs were against the wall." That is when they were going through the storms of life.

Our God is great; He is majestic and all-powerful. He is loving and kind! He is the incredible God that deserves incredible praise. He is all-sufficient yet more than enough. He is the God of a second chance. He is the restorer of the breach. He is the Lily of the Valley and the Bright Morning Star. He is the Ancient of Days! He is the great High Priest and the I Am that I am. He is the wheel in the middle of the wheel. He is the fairest of ten thousand and the Bright Morning Star. He is all of these and so much more.

So then, friend, what are you experiencing today? What do you need to experience at the hand of God? Turn your eyes to Him! Cry out, and He will hear and deliver you. There is hope in *King Jesus*; there is hope in *God*. Turn your eyes to the hills from whence cometh your help. He gives hope to the hopeless and grace in their times of need.

> But they that wait upon the LORD shall renew their strength; they shall mount up with wings as eagles; they shall run, and not be weary; and they shall walk, and not faint. (Isaiah 40:31)

Declaration

I am surrounded by the power and might of God. I am more than a conqueror through the blood of Jesus Christ. I overcome every circumstance of life that presents itself against me in the Mighty Name of Jesus Christ of Nazareth!

GOD IS INTENTIONAL ABOUT YOUR LIFE

The children of Israel were few in comparison to the nations around them. They were, however, the apple of God's eyes. Despite their many shortcomings and afflictions, they were a chosen generation. They had the mark of God on their lives, and nothing was allowed to hold them back. All they needed to do was to trust and obey Him, and their path would be as the shining light.

My friend, even the devil knew the lines that he could not cross. He understood that there was no way he could touch them unless they walked away from the covenant of the Most High God.

Unfortunate for them, they rebelled against God. As a means of punishment, they were allowed to be taken into bondage by the Egyptians: they remained in captivity for four hundred years. During this period, they worked as slaves and suffered greatly. When they cried to God, He heard their distress and sent Moses to their rescue. Once He got ready to deliver them, the children of Israel went out with boldness in the sight of all the Egyptians. Though they were slaves, they did not have to shrink out of Egypt. God gave them the boldness to leave as conquerors, not as escaping slaves.

So what is the benefit of surrendering fully to God? There are several of them, in fact, too many to count. He is not joking when He says that He wants to be your Father. He is intentional about your life. He seeks a deep and permanent relationship with you. Jesus desires to set you high above all limitations. He plans to bless you and give you an expected end.

My friend, hear me, and hear me very well; this is your season of intimacy with God! It's your season of deep relationship with

Him! My friend, it's your season of boldness. Please remember that the people who know their God shall be strong and do exploits. It does not matter what has happened in your past; it does not matter where you have been. You can get into a relationship with God today. Make Him your Lord and Father and receive power to mount up with wings like an eagle. Receive the power of God to run and not be weary! In the name of Jesus, you shall walk and not faint.

My friend, fear not, have no doubt! Trust God and allow Him to lead you beyond your today. Let Him lead you into His path of righteousness. Fear not for though others have failed you, He will not fail nor forsake you. He sticks closer than a brother and is faithful to them that put their trust in Him. Give him a chance today, and your life will never be the same.

> Be strong and of a good courage, fear not,
> nor be afraid of them: for the LORD thy God, he
> *it is* that doth go with thee; he will not fail thee,
> nor forsake thee. (Deuteronomy 31:6)

Declaration

I am purpose-driven. I fulfill God's plan for my life daily. With fearlessness, I shall execute all my God-given assignments.

THE CRY THAT TOUCHES THE HEART OF GOD

This poor man cried. Have you ever cried "that cry," or at least, when have you last cried that cry? You have been crying, but how and to whom? Something is interesting about a cry that reaches the heart of God. This is a desperate cry! A cry which penetrates all barriers, transcends all hurdles, and boomerangs into the very presence of God.

Yes, friend, this cry is such that it bypasses all sounds and amid all else connects with God. God's concern is for our hearts. He wants us to be honest with him. Blind Bartimaeus made such a cry as Jesus approached him. There was much to do and chattering, but his cry drowned out all else, and Jesus heard him. The woman, with the issue of blood, silently made that cry. She was at the right place at the wrong time. She had stepped away from protocols and programs because of her need. Even though she did not speak, her heart was heard because she made a cry! Similarly to Bartimaeus, her cry was sincere, but whereas his was loud, hers was silently gut-wrenching and desperate. This desperate cry was what prompted her to make a healing touch. When Jesus heard these cries, He had no choice but to act.

David himself, a wealthy king, indicated that this poor man cried, and God heard him and delivered him from all his troubles. Was David poor financially? No, but he was distraught. In spirit, he was a very distressed man. He was perplexed and confused and needed a savior. His friends became his enemies, and those that hated him had increased. He needed God's intervention, and he needed it urgently. He was at the breaking point of his life. His feet were now slipping, and his hope was in a precarious position. His troubles had reduced him to a *poor* state, one which spoke to destitution and despair. This was when he made a cry, such as he had never made before. This kind of cry got God's attention. All these individuals felt as though they were faced with more than they could bear, though God *Himself* promised not to give any of us more than we can bear. We know God is faithful, so it was the devil and his oppression that caused these individuals to feel the way they felt.

Friend, there comes the point in every man's life when he must recognize that he needs God's intervention. He must know that he cannot survive without making that cry! This cry is not necessarily loud, though it may be. This cry is not joyous but has to come from a place of pain and desperation to be heard.

What is your situation today? Let God hear your voice. Cry out, and He will deliver you from the troubles you are experiencing. He is waiting for you. Seek Him and believe His word. He is for you, not against you. He awaits your approach right now. Reach out and touch Him, and you will never be the same, in Jesus' name.

> This poor man cried and the LORD heard *him,* and saved him out of all his troubles. (Psalm 34:6)

Declaration

God hears me when I pray. I'm always on His mind, and He has great plans for my life. I receive my deliverance and walk in freedom by the blood of Jesus Christ of Nazareth.

JOIN FORCE WITH THE COVENANT-KEEPING GOD

God is not a man, so *He cannot lie*! *He* never changes His mind, neither does He disappoints. *His* character is impeccable. By virtue of *His* flawless nature, *His* reputation precedes *Him* as being unquestionably and undeniably trustworthy.

God is our Creator. *His* love for us is measureless and indescribable. The closest reflection of God's love is that of an earthy father for his children. To draw a clear illustration of *His* love and providential care for us, *His* creation, He referred to our earthy father granting the request of his children (Matthew 7:9–11). God's love for *His* creation is what causes *Him* to pity us every time, despite our sinful nature. We can never do any work that will merit *His* love, but still, *He* loves us so much that while we were yet in sin, Christ died for us. He who knew no sin became sin for us to make us joint-heirs in the kingdom of God.

Beloved friend, God loves you. His love for you is unconditional. He loves you with an everlasting love. Because of this love, He will do His good pleasure in you. Of course, the devil knows all of this, and his aim daily is to turn your heart away from God. He is aware that if you truly understand God's love and provincial care, he will lose ground. He knows that if we know how much God truly cares for and has our best interest at heart, he has no opportunity to prevail against us. That is the reason why he seeks to put a veil over our eyes when given the opportunity. He is a deceiver and the father of all lies. This is why it is not hard for him to fabricate a story or trick us by deception. *He* also strives to manipulate our minds in a quest to bait and draw us away from God. The moment we become relentless and resist him, he has to flee from us.

So be honest with me, what do you desire? For what are you longing? Is it in the word of God—the *Bible*? If that is the case, then rest assured that He will do it! *God* is not a man that He should lie. *God* is incapable of lying. Period! It is against *His* nature to break a promise made to you. *He* is the only good covenant-keeping God, and as such, you can rely on *Him*. You can trust *Him* to bring your desires to pass. Nothing will *He* withhold from those who walk uprightly.

Do you know what He said in His words? "Cast your cares upon me because I care for you. Commit your ways unto Me, trust Me, and I will bring your desires to pass. Delight yourself also in Me, and I will give you the desires of your heart."

Does that sound like authenticity? What about integrity and capability? How about throwing accountability into the mix? God is all of the above and so much more. Trust Him to supply your needs. Trust Him to bring your expectations to pass! Believe Him on the basis that your requests are in sync with His will. If that is the case, He will do it.

Faithful *is* he that calls you, who also will do *it.* (1 Thessalonians 5:24)

Declaration

Today I dare to believe God and take Him at His word. I walk boldly into my inheritance, knowing that the One who has called me is faithful. He will perfect that which concerns me.

JESUS, ROCK IN A WEARY LAND

Hey there, friend, how are you doing? Have you ever been walking and suddenly felt an overpowering surge of tiredness and a rock in the distance came to your rescue? Have you ever been traveling with a large bag and someone lent you a helping hand at what you would consider your breaking point? What about the time when you had a very pressing situation that caused you sleepless nights and you finally decided to seek advice. At the point of doing so, you felt relief even when all you might have gotten was a listening ear.

Everyone needs a rock at some point in their journey. Whatever your time of day is, a rock is always a source of deliverance. These pillars of support are usually so reliable that you find them in the same spot. It means, therefore, that if you travel to a certain location over a period, you are likely to see the same rock. Short of a blast or some natural disasters such as an earthquake or volcano, a rock remains irremovable for hundreds of years.

My friend, your spiritual Rock is Jesus Christ. There is grace enough in *Him* for every need, but you must avail yourself of it. In this life, you must know that there will be many hardships. The reason for this is because the god of this world, satan, is determined to afflict man and beasts alike. Yes, you got it correct—life is a battlefield, and that is why you need the *Rock* of ages. He is reliable, constant, and can never fail.

If you are a soldier of the cross, your one aim should be to please this *Rock* who recruited you to *His* army. In order to be all that he would have you to be, you must avoid entangling yourself in all civilian matters. As a soldier, you must remain in barracks in Christ

Jesus, where military personnel are quartered, and from which they may, at any hour, be summoned to duty. The reason for this is that the less encumbered you are, the more quickly you will execute the commands of your Lord and Savior.

Yes, friend, it is an honor to be enlisted as a soldier in the Lord's army. It is incredible to have him as your supportive Rock and army general! However, what if you are not yet recruited? If you have not enlisted as yet, my mission is to remind you that He is calling you to Himself. His arms are outstretched, and He is patiently waiting for you to become militant. In short, He wants you to know that He desperately loves you and desires a deep and everlasting relationship with you. Once you embrace this journey, you will find that it's a race to the finish line—eternity.

Oh yes, friend, as God becomes your rock, you find that life is like an amphitheater. It is filled with celestial spectators who are cheering you on to success. This race to eternity is of paramount importance. No one can stop midway and inherit the prize given to all winners. The beautiful thing, however, is that this race is not for the swift but for all those who dare to finish it.

Here is the sad reality, however: you may be your worst antagonist without knowing it. Many have failed miserably in this race because they allowed themselves to be derailed, but I assure you that there is hope! Take a step by faith today, develop a spiritual diet, exercise purity, study the manual for daily living, and you will lay hold on eternal life. Run your race then, friend; sit or stand on the Rock as the daily need arises, and you will wear a crown someday.

> Thou therefore, my son, be strong in the grace that is in Christ Jesus. And the things that thou hast heard of me among many witnesses, the same commit thou to faithful men, who shall be able to teach others also. Thou therefore endure hardness, as a good soldier of Jesus Christ. No man that wars entangles himself with the affairs

of this life; that he may please him who hath chosen him to be a soldier. (2 Timothy 2:1–4)

Declaration

I am a soldier in the Lord's army! I run my race patiently, and
by His grace, I will one day lay hold on eternal life.

CALLED TO CONQUER AND OVERCOME

My beloved friend, just as there is a physical world with real people, communities, enterprises, and the likes that you can see—there is a spiritual world! This is the world that God and angels occupy. Unfortunately, this is also the world in which satan and his demons exist because they too are spirits.

Though these worlds have been in existence since the beginning of time (for the physical) and before time began (for the spiritual), some have not been able to tap into or understand the mysteries of the spiritual world. It is not surprising to discover, therefore, that many people believe it's delusional. This would not have been a major issue if that very ideology was not exactly what satan wanted them to believe. As a deceiver, he knows that if he tricks all human beings into believing that he doesn't exist, the blames for evil and wrongdoings will be placed at the wrong feet. To make it plain and simple, the fewer people know about him, his operations, and the reality that he is the mastermind behind life's destruction and distractions, the less they'll blame him for their troubles, and therefore, accuse God. Oh yes, most people know him to be the accuser of the brethren, but very few know that he is also the accuser of the Lord Jesus Christ.

Have you ever heard the things people ask regarding God as they contemplate suffering and pain among humanity? Yes, countless people question His very existence and whether or not He cares about the work of His hand—His Creation. This occurs due to a lack of knowledge and understanding of the existence and operation of the supernatural. Within this world, there are constant wars that gradually manifest themselves in the physical world. Good against evil and evil against good. These combats intensify as the end draws nearer. Of course, the war was instigated by satan in heaven and has been continuous since his forceful eviction.

Everything that manifests in the physical realm or world therefore first existed in the spirit realm. The evil one—satan—continues to oppress mankind, God's creation, in the quest to retaliate against God. As a result, man is daily tempted to sin against his Maker's commandments. Being a vindictive foe, the devil does not relent, and man must therefore fight until he draws his last breath.

Do you believe that there is power over sin and hell? Yes, it is clearly indicated throughout the scriptures that we are meant to overcome. As the Apostle Paul sat within the confines of a prison cell, he classified himself as a prisoner for Christ. He explained that nothing could separate us from the love of God. By those words, He actually meant that no condition *at all* could separate the believer from Jesus Christ.

I, therefore, like to call this particular passage of Romans "The Warrior's Manual." It is here that we see in an even more profound way that we are more than conquerors. We are meant to battle life and win it. We are designed with war in mind.

In closing his argument, the apostle shows that believers are dear to God because they are in Christ. Their every need have been anticipated and are already provided for; their guilt has been canceled and provision made for their holy and victorious character. The Holy Spirit is accessible to all those that believe, and God is fighting for them forever.

Dear friend, you who are reading, I am speaking to you. Seeing the exceedingly great and matchless way in which Christ loves you, who or what will you truly allow to separate you from the love of God in Christ Jesus? What shall separate you from Christ? Shall tribulation, distress, persecution, famine, nakedness, peril, or sword? No way, even the most extreme situation cannot affect how God feels about you, so don't pull away from Him. Don't forget, for one moment, that He loves you like no other.

Indeed, all the operations of hell cannot separate you from God if you do not allow it. The devil, principalities, powers, and all rulers of darkness cannot stop God from loving you. In order to know and experience this love, however, you must be united to the Lord Jesus by living faith. Then, and only then, will you be more than a conqueror—that is, you shall not only be victorious but shall get spoil out of the very things that were designed to have hurt you.

> Nay, in all these things we are more than conquerors through him that loved us. (Romans 8:37)

Declaration

I am more than a conqueror through the blood of Jesus Christ. I am strong, indomitable, and invincible by the power of Him, who has called me to live the victorious life. It's not I but Christ within me who causes me to defeat every representative of the gates of hell.

THE PAST IS OVER

"The past is over" is an overrated phrase you may say, my friend. It is so often used that we wonder about its meaning. This is because, despite its usage, many people are still shackled by their past. Day by day, they relive the memories of lost dreams, hopes, and aspirations. Many of them are so trapped that, like a wounded animal, they have great difficulty embracing the newness of life. Indeed, many more people inhabit the bubbles of the past than they live in their present lives. Many individuals, while their time away comparing the present to the past, thus, becoming too crippled, even to make significant life decisions.

To transcend to the next phase of their lives, many people have successfully placed a bandage over past hurts, pain, shame, and disappointments. As these bandages are forcefully removed, perhaps by friends, relatives, or other close associates, they recognize the pains and rejections based on the action and words of the one plagued by the past.

Take for example an adult who grew up in a dysfunctional home, which included abuse and or poverty. You know this individual has not recovered from past pains based on his or her reaction toward life's matters. A person who suffers rejection may still be living in the past based on how he or she treats people, even after he or she changes location. In reality, though, can we change our past? That is a simple question that can be complex depending on the temperament, culture, and even beliefs of the offended. Friend, I believe that the past can become a thing of the past if it is effectively addressed. No matter how offended we have been, we must find a way to make peace with our past so we can enjoy our present and future.

The easiest way to get over the haunts, guilts, fears, and frustrations of the past is to first identify it. We must identify the root of our problems, come to terms with our realities, and deal with them accordingly. We never overcome situations that we shove under a rug. As often as we walk on that surface, there will always be an uneven bump. The way forward, therefore, is acknowledging and releasing ourselves from it. We must face our past and deal with it.

For me, talking is quite therapeutic. I like to face the person who hurts me and let him or her know how I feel. During this time, I try, as much as possible, to use "I" messages. For example, I will say to the offender, "I felt that way when you did or said this or that to me…" (relay the situation here).

If you hate confrontations, you may need to write a message, make a telephone call, or even send an e-mail. The bottom line is that you will need to identify the situation, determine how it makes you feel, and deal with it. What if the person is unreachable due to death or relocation, you may ask. Well, you still need a release. The foremost thing is prayer, but remember that you can write a journal. As you do, create a balance: write what happened, how it affected you, and what you have learnt from the incident. Always end on a positive note since you must ensure this hold over you is broken.

Once you identify the source of hurt or pain, etc., own up to wherever you may have been in the wrong. This is your history; it is your past. You cannot change your past, but it does not have to cripple you. My friend, you must bear in mind that what is done is already done, and you cannot undo it. Yes, it's true that this is easier said than done, but be honest with me, what can you do about spilled milk? You can only mop it up and move forward. The only time you can be free of your past is when you grapple with it and overcome it.

In retrospect, what did you learn from this or those past experiences? Once you acknowledge and accept the past, you are now in a position to take valuable lessons from it. Your past does not have to destroy you; you can study it and use it to guide you into the future. No matter what you do, do not internalize bad habits and anxieties—only practical lessons. You may not be able to undo what happened, but you might be able to keep it from happening again.

Bear in mind that you cannot change certain things. For example, I met a precious lady once who confided in me that her son was conceived after she was raped. For her, the child is a reminder of this incident. This is not any easy situation, but this mother can help both herself and her child by understanding that both of them are truly victims who can become victorious. She has to recognize that she did not deserve to be raped and the child did not cause what happened. In spite of this being a very painful ordeal, much good can be derived from such relationship, if it is properly handled.

Another, and the most effective, way in which I deal with my past is through prayer. To God be the glory that I have discovered that all my help comes from Him. I grew up under adverse circumstances, but I did not allow them to break me. In fact, I have become very strong because of these experience and have even become a tower of strength to others due to my experiences. Now, when I look over my life, I say like David, "Lord, it was good that I was afflicted because I learnt to pay greater attention to your word." My storms have made me weatherproof.

My friend, no matter what pain from your past continues to resurface and bring you grief, you can overcome that situation. You can be delivered! You can be healed and set free. If counseling or therapies are not helping you, I know for sure that Jesus can heal you. He is the best mender of broken hearts. He heals present, past, and future pain, and He sets the captives free. Give them all to Jesus, and *He* will turn your mourning into dancing. He will turn your sorrows into joy.

> Brethren, I do not count myself to have apprehended; but one thing *I do,* forgetting those things which are behind and reaching forward to those things which are ahead. (Philippians 3:13)

Declaration

I am no longer a prisoner of my past. I am delivered from every shackle of mistakes, pains, hurts, and traumas. I am victorious, and I prevail spiritually, physically, emotionally, financially, and emotionally.

THERE IS NO CONDEMNATION

As the notorious criminal was led into the courtroom, he hung his head in shame and derision. His shoulder drooped, hopelessly. He could barely see the floor as he wearily placed one foot before the other.

Not only was he guilty of the crime he was charged for, but he could also hear the never-ending shrill cry of the last victim. Perhaps it was the eyes, which pleaded with him, that intensified his torture now. Hadn't he been tormented enough? He had lost count of the many crimes and victims, but this one was different; it was probably the worst case. He would remember it, to his grave.

His Grammy often told him fancy stories on a balmy Sunday evening during their alone time on the back step of their cozy, rambling, old house. This was probably the only place where he ever felt or experienced love. *Isn't it funny*, he thought to himself now, *how the ones that truly love you never stay around long enough to see you through the dismal days.* Grammy used to say memories don't live as people do; they always remember you. He tried, unsuccessfully, to replace the drab memories of his latest crime with a striking image of his dear, precious grandmother. He even tried to whisper a prayer as he thought back to the day she first taught him the "Our Father" prayer. That was years ago. He could not even remember the date.

He did not believe he deserved mercy; however, he still prayed. Grammy always told him that there was hope for every last prayer if the person praying believed. Back then, he believed more: Yes, he was more hopeful, but now, he felt as though the cord of hope was getting shorter and shorter. *May her soul rest in peace*, he thought. For some reason, memories of her gentle voice and warm touch flooded his thought all morning. Even as he shuffled his way along the dingy corridors that led into the courtroom.

He hardly recognized himself these days. How could he, an ardent Sunday school student and later a teacher with an immaculate persona, have become such an atrocious and brutish individual!

As he listened to the chains jangling from his feet, his mind drifted to that fateful night. Every step he took appeared as if a blow landed against his subconscious mind. He was betwixt a rock and a hard place, and he knew it was no one's fault but his.

The silence in the courtroom was palpable. It was almost deafening but worse was the stench of condemnation and the thick cloud of hatred that though invisible to others, hung heavily over him.

A hoarse cough woke him from his daydream as he realized that it was once more time to face the judge, the one in whose hands his fate hung. He was told that he would probably qualify for early parole if he kept up the good behavior. He knew he did not deserve clemency. Perhaps, however, "the One" grandma and his Sunday school teacher spoke so lustrously about, the One who dwelt in the heavens, would have mercy upon him and help set him free.

Should he be set free? He was the first to acknowledge that, indeed, he did not deserve such luxury. He had lived a life of crime. He deserved his punishment, but if only…

As he miserably mulled his situation, he recognized that a lull had fallen over the otherwise buzzing room. There had been an uproar upon his arrival, as though everyone wanted to eat him alive. Soon, however, things were hushed as the clerk of the court shouted, "Order in the court." He could almost touch the tension and hatred that dripped in the courtroom. His breathing was beginning to grow labored, and the panic attack threatened to overpower him. He felt the first wave of nausea and knew, without a doubt, that the dark, fainting spell that had become his new companion was going to overwhelm him. Just before its vicious claw made the final hold, just before he lost it completely, he heard a booming voice say, "Set him free. I will take his place!"

Does the narrative above sound familiar, my friend? "Certainly not…I am not a criminal," you may say. Indeed, you would not be wrong, but while your story and mine may be different, the story line is the same. We have all fallen short in this life. We have all done wrong things. I cannot tell you how many times I have made decisions that I had no business making. I did things that were wrong. I should have paid the price, but Jesus did it for me! He did it for you! He took the death we deserved and paid the price that we owed. He set us free.

Friend, be reminded that the enemy (satan) is constantly accusing you and me before God. He brings every mistake we make to the forefront. He torments us by whispering to our spirit day and night. Not only are we faced with the challenges of our daily life, but the guilty conscience is a terror from time to time. The reason why I know this is because I have been there! You are probably at that place too.

I remember being tormented for mistakes I made. I remember having very long and sleepless nights as I twisted and turned in my bed. I remember praying, but at times, I felt as though I was not forgiven. I remember wondering if it made any sense living.

My friend, I also remember when I surrendered my life to Jesus. I was mocked and jeered. I was called names, and for sure, I was given an allotted time by which I was going to move away from the presence of God. They said I was not going to make it in life.

My father died the year I was born, and I had no peace as a child growing up. It was bad enough that I was born to a married man, but what made things worse was that I thought, he chose to die shortly after my birth. I grew up wondering if that was why no one could love me. I thought I was cursed. Things were difficult, and my mother, who was abused, did not know how to show love. She has four of us, all for different men, and my stepfather, to whom she was married, was not the father of any of us. She always told us how miserable her life had been and still was during his lifetime. To me, he was the sweetest human being, though he too had faults, but they never got along. She always told me that she regretted having kids. She would often tell me that though I was such a good child to her, she had difficulty dealing with me since I resembled my father very much. She would also tell me that he mistreated her and had promised to marry her, which he, of course, did not do.

Overall, my existence was a continued reminder of a man who had failed my mother on many levels. Being a product of such dysfunctional family dynamics was hard. I continued to have various hardships over the years. I keep going on, but I desperately wanted to die. I had gotten to the point of great depression and frustration. That was when I contemplated ending my life. Well, God had other plans for me. He saved me. He gave me an amazing husband, and today, I am living victoriously. Oh yes, Jesus came to my rescue. I was a prisoner of my circumstances. I was not a criminal but was often treated like one. I had no idea who I was until Jesus stepped in one day and said, "My child, take my hand, and I will give you new life." He gave me beauty for ashes. He removed the garment of shame and condemnation and placed on me a new robe and a crown of excellence and glory.

I am now living in the full understanding and assurance that there is no condemnation to me, who is in Christ Jesus. I am a child of God. I am a royal princess. I am peculiar, and I tell it wherever I go. I am delivered and set free.

My friend, today can be your day! My friend, today can be the start of a new beginning in your life. What have you done? How far have you gone? Is an inner voice telling you, you have sinned, there is no use to pray? Were you once walking with Jesus but turned away from his loving care? You are chosen, and once chosen, God is the judge, and you stand before him with an accuser next to you. Next to the judge, however, is your advocate, the one who will speak for you. When the accuser brings a charge against you, the advocate will tell the judge, "This is the one for whom I have died. His penalty is paid." At that point, all charges against you have to be dropped. Receive freedom and walk in victory today, in Jesus's name.

Who shall lay anything to the charge of
God's elect? It is God that justified. (Romans 8:33)

Declaration

I am free from condemnation and oppression. I am surrounded by blessings. My life is a testimony of the favour of God!

SAY NO TO MEDIOCRITY

Friend, in a world that is on a fast track to apparent destruction, one in which most things are allowed or accepted, I know you sometimes ask the question, "Do I still stand a chance?" Is it all right to stand for something, or should I fall for anything? Should I fight against mediocrity or fall into the *"Relax, everybody is doing it" mode*?

I am confident that the term "mediocrity" is not new to you. It is a word that has pronounced actions and which has become quite prevalent in its manifestation. In fact, in many instances, it appears that more people embrace indifference or ordinariness. Mediocrity is observed on a greater level among the younger generation. It is something that must be eradicated from our lives, my friend, if we are going to be the trendsetters and trailblazers that we are meant to be.

Let us examine quite briefly how this is seen and its impact or likely impact. Let us start with my field of endeavors—teaching. As you know, the classroom is not the first place of learning; however, much formal learning takes place there. I have noticed that the system has begun to embrace the spirit of mediocrity in a very bad way. I know you understand why I say *spirit*. You already know that there are two worlds—a spiritual and a physical one. All things that you see physically first manifest in the spirit before they manifest in the physical. Of course, the spirit world or realm comprises of spirits as much as the physical realm comprises of human beings. Spirits can navigate any of the two realms, as they have a mind, through the vortexes of the earth. Since there are good (angels) spirits and bad (demons and fallen angels) spirits, there are constant activities in the spirit realm. Remember, the devil rules the bad spirits and is the greatest archenemy of God, his maker and the ruler of the universe. One of the strategies that this evil devil uses against humanity is the operation of mediocrity. He is aware that a person, who knows his full potential and walks therein, is a lethal weapon against him. Why is this, you may ask. Well, every vessel of honor to God is a force to be reckoned with by the gates of hell. You can, therefore, understand why the devil assigns the spirit of mediocrity to all humanity.

So let us go back to talking about the system: The devil is, knowingly or unknowingly, manipulating many world leaders and policymakers. As a result, laws are being changed and others implemented to enforce specific regulation and rights throughout the land. A prime example is the education system in many societies. This one has subtly been encouraging tardiness. As a result, many youngsters are no longer being pushed to be their best, work harder, or be better than yesterday. Here it has become quite alarming and distressful that based on all the different feelings, emotions, and rights to be protected, laxness, careless and even poor performance are seen as acceptable and sometimes a given.

Things have gotten so very *out of hand* that it is no longer acceptable to correct students' underperformance, lest the rights of children or learners are jeopardized, as their emotions will be affected. Because they have several rights, teachers must tiptoe around their poor performance, lest they are penalized and punished by stringent measures. It is a battle that can be won if you and I will take a stand. We are not holding them accountable by allowing young people to see everything as a direct insult. I have always been resolute not to encourage a student to cry "Unfair!" when he failed a subject as a result of his tardiness.

Let us look at athletics; in many instances and events, all participants are distinguished and awarded highly. Some, therefore, embrace the idea that excellence is no longer the prerequisite for reward. As a result, the bars are lowered, and everyone knows that the requirement for reward is mere participation. I can see you nodding in agreement, my friend. Indeed, many people do not pay attention to excellence. "Well, of course," they say, "we are entitled because we were involved!" Not "we are awarded for outstanding performance" but "we are awarded for engaging in" or at least "attempting." Of course, since mediocrity is highly celebrated worldwide, why does anyone have to do his best anymore? Well, that appears to be the question in many strata of life.

Indeed, indifference has become so prevalent that people are comfortable settling for leasing, and many are not putting their best foot forward for themselves, their family, and the people around them, and this is quite disheartening. What this means is that people are encouraged to stay in their comfort zone.

I will not endorse or celebrate mediocrity, and neither should you. Excellence is still God's way. Even as I wrote this book, I was determined that this would not be another book. I could not merely settle for the mundane. I needed to know that this book would forever impact your life.

If you have children, are a pastor, a leader of an organization, or simply an influence of any kind, teach your people to try harder, run farther, and pull through. Reward those who do not just coast on easy success but see an opportunity and give it their all. *It is okay not to be the best.* However, it is not okay not to try. Encourage them not to celebrate just making it through but celebrate when they have overcome or gone above and beyond. What am I saying? I repeat, do not celebrate mediocrity! Do not embrace or encourage yourself or anyone else to just pass the day doing a task or living life. Be the best of whom you were created to be. Is there a song in your belly? Is there a book, or are their books to be written? My friend, what is the gift that God, your Creator, has given unto you? Please, I beg of you, do the best you can to manifest it. Make it known on a level of excellence.

> Verily, verily, I say unto you, He that believeth
> on me, the works that I do shall he do also; and
> greater *works* than these shall ye do. (John 14:12)

Declaration

Through God, my Creator, I improve on all assigned tasks daily! I am greater than my most excellent assignment. I do all things remarkably and outstandingly well. I do nothing ordinary, which is because God's plan for me is great and mighty.

AUTUMN

SEASON OF CONFIDENCE

Hey, friend, have you ever heard that confidence is everything? So what is confidence? Confidence is the feeling of self-assurance arising from one's appreciation of one's abilities or qualities.

It is not always about escaping the den but sometimes being thrown in for what you believe, maintaining your belief, and coming out all right by God's grace.

Some people will tell you that you are a person of resilience when you overcome struggles and rise even though you have fallen many times. For me, however, that is more than resilience. That is confidence because you hope against hope and fought your way back to a standing position. Though life tried to beat you to the ground and trample you, you dared to stand tall amid the heartaches and distresses.

To be secure means you know it is okay to face severe tests. To be confident means you understand that the more frequently difficulties come, the stronger you get, and one day, you will be triumphant. To be confident means you know that outcome, whatever it may be, is just that: an outcome. It's also an understanding that once that outcome passes, there will be another opportunity in whatever way it presents itself for you to create a new result.

To be confident means you don't always smile. To be confident means the circumstances that were meant to break you build you. To be confident doesn't mean you never cry, but for every tear shed, you know laughter awaits.

Dear friend, having confidence in "yourself" is not arrogance, but you will indeed possess inner peace, even in adverse circumstances. This posture also allows you to know that all is well regarding a particular matter. Confidence in yourself is also an indication that you are aware of your assignment. Confidence is being aware of your weaknesses and being certain that someday, they can become your strengths.

So then, as quoted by Roy T. Bennett,

> Don't let the expectations and opinions of other people affect your decisions: It's your life, not theirs. Do what matters most to you; do what makes you feel alive and happy. Don't let the expectations and ideas of others limit who you are. If you let others tell you who you are, you are living their reality—not yours. There is more to life than pleasing people. There is much more to life than following others' prescribed path. There is so much more to life than what you experience right now. You need to decide who you are for yourself. Become a whole being Adventure.

My friend, confidence is mainly attainable through the power and grace of God. Today, therefore, I encourage you to cast your cares upon Jesus. Look unto Him, the Author and Finisher of your faith. Embrace His word and mandate for your life. It is He that made you. He cares for you. He is willing to contend for your life. Walk in boldness and confidence, knowing that *He* will not rest until the best version of you is manifested.

> Being confident of this very thing, that he which hath begun a good work in you will perform it until the day of Jesus Christ. (Philippians 1:6)

Declaration

I am grateful for the skills and talents with which God has blessed me. I see life as a very precious and beautiful commodity. I am therefore happy to be alive today. I am succeeding daily as I remain humble yet confident.

THE VALLEY—YOUR PLACE OF RESTORATION

Before David became the *king* of Israel, he was first and foremost a *shepherd* boy. He was required to spend quality time with the sheep. As a shepherd, his role was of a dual nature. On the one hand, David was blessed with the task of nurturing the sheep as they were born. On the other, he was faced with the mammoth task of warding off predators and all kinds of enemies that lurked around, especially in the dark.

While David enjoyed watching his flock increase, he had to deal with the responsibilities that every good shepherd has. His task included tending to wounded sheep, finding the best watering holes, and ensuring that none died during birth or at the jaws of predators. From all indications, the job of a shepherd was not an easy one.

The scriptures never, at any point, indicated that David had a physical helper. As I wrote this for you, my friend, I began to wonder, what might have been his plight on the days when he felt weary or sick? While pondering this question, I heard the words "*divine provision*" quite audibly. As David's flock grew, so should his concern, but God was with him.

Life as a shepherd, for David, proved quite dangerous and posed various perils. Between dealing with injured sheep and those that fell into ravines or lost their way, he had quite a bit to do. That meant, therefore, that he had to be quite strategic with planning rescue missions and implementing safety measures as the flock increased. In addition, he had to locate grassy terrains and ensure that they were well watered. After a while of shepherding the sheep, he became a master at his craft.

On two separate occasions, David was faced with the challenge of standing up to a lion and a bear. These were no easy feats, but because God was with him, he slew both with his bare hands. As David cared for his flock, he soon learnt the art of consistency and defense mechanism. He also learnt about and rejected the option of being a hireling. David knew that the hireling did his job for personal benefits and gains while the shepherd tended the sheep for their own sake. David chose the latter. In the face of danger, he chose to stand and did his best to defend his sheep. Not once did he, as the hireling did, consider his own safety and protection above that of the sheep.

As he tended to the sheep, he himself required tending, and soon he learnt that when nobody was there, God was there. The backside of the desert can be arid and lonely. Most likely, the light of the moon was his guide to get home on many balmy nights. There were likely desert storms and all sorts of natural elements, with which he had to contend.

When no one was around, David learnt to compose songs and sung these to his God. As he did, a most fantastic thing began brewing: He learnt to depend on the God of his Fathers. David started to have his own experiences with God. As he tended the sheep, he found out that God, his God, was tending to his need. David soon recognized that there were seen and unseen dangers in a desert, but he was kept safe. He soon realized that his protection was not due to his skillfulness but as a result of God's constant intervention in his life.

As David attended to his flock, he knew fully well what it was like to feel down and out. He knew what it was like to be discouraged. These, for him, were the valley moments. He soon recognized, however, that no matter what happened, he was never truly alone.

Being a shepherd, David, from time to time, required a rod and a staff. The rod was used as a weapon of protection for him and the sheep. He also used it as a support system while he walked. The staff had a crook. Its significance was that of hooking sheep going astray or that had fallen off the path.

By His mystical power, God began to reveal himself as David's shepherd. As David's life took on new meaning and dimension, it became clear that no one understood God's staff and rod as much as he did.

Do you recall the word *God* gave me earlier in this passage "*DIVINE PROVISION*"? As David used those physical tools and reflected on his role in the sheep's lives, he saw how God directed him along life's paths. David saw the "shepherdship" of God unfurl before his eyes. He recognized that it was God's rod of correction and his staff that drew him back to the fold every time he sinned or fell from grace.

David loved God, and despite his many faults and shortcoming, he held a special place in God's heart to the point where God declared him to be a man after *His* own heart. Why is that? You may ask. Well, from his youth, God saw Himself in David. God saw his genuine love and concern for his flock as well as for people. He saw David's love for justice and his concern for the underprivileged. He saw a replica of Himself in David. David, on the other hand, saw God manifesting Himself on His behalf. He saw the many times God preserved him from death and the grave. He understood that had it not been for God on his side, he would have been consumed by his enemies and those who professed to be his friend. Though many dangers and perils assailed him, David knew he needed not fear because he was never alone. *God*, his *God*, was with him, and so he knew that no matter what happened, his life would not go to waste.

As David's sheep trusted their lives to him, so David mastered the art of depending on his good shepherd. He knew from whence his help came! He knew who would correct him when he had sinned! He knew who cared to get him back on track when he had fallen off the trail of life! David knew that no matter how deep in trouble he was, *God* would never fail nor forsake him! What a relationship, what a trust?

The physical valley was one that David knew well. You see, friend, the valley is a low area of land between hills or mountains, typically with a river or stream flowing through it. This was a good place to rest, water the flock, and tend to wounded or sick sheep. As David looked back, he recognized that it had to be God that delivered him from the jaws of the lion and the paws of the bear. In retrospect, he concluded that God was to him, what he was to his sheep—his good shepherd.

As time went by and David saw all the traps and enemy pits he escaped, his confidence grew. He recognized that many times he could have and should have died, but God kept him. David realized that through God, all death traps were mere shadows and not the real thing. David experienced many valley experiences, but continually, God restored his soul.

Where are you at this stage of your life? What is God to you? If *He* is your Good Shepherd, you need not be afraid. No matter how dark the path of life becomes, you need not be scared. No matter how complex the challenges are, you are not alone! God will be your rear reward. Trust *Him* today and allow *Him* to take you through every valley of loneliness, hopelessness, and despair. Allow him to lead you through any valley you are navigating right now, and remember, the valley is a place for restoration. The valley is a place of repairing and renovating. Invite Him in today, and He will be whatever you want *Him* to be to you in the mighty and exalted name of *Jesus Christ of Nazareth*.

> Yea, though I walk through the valley of the shadow of death, I will fear no evil: for thou art with me; thy rod and thy staff they comfort me. (Psalm 23:4)

Declaration

I am never alone! I am surrounded by the blood of Jesus and the fire of God. Jesus, my Good Shepherd, and my Jehovah Jireh, knows and supplies all my needs. He loads me daily with benefits.

BE TRUE TO YOUR CALLING

Insecurity and inferiority have removed many of significance and relevance from the presence of God. As a result of such contaminants, these people have lost their anointing and suffered great ruin. In the quest to fulfill selfish ambitions and gratify self-seeking ventures, these people lost sight of the reality that the one who anointed and called them to serve was able to keep them from falling. As they walked on the broad road of men's approval, they failed to see that lucifer had become their guide. They never learnt the art of pleasing God, thus settling comfortably into their gifts and calling. They refused to run the race with patience and with an emphasis on pleasing Christ. In the mad rush to impress people, they failed to recognize the main thing—that God is a respecter of no man and shall pay every man according as his work shall be.

One such individual was King Saul. He was selected and anointed by God and placed as king over the nation of Israel. Though Saul's position was secure in God, he was greatly plagued by the spirits of insecurity and inferiority. He was so insecure about his position within the hearts of the people that he became a slave to them. Twice he admitted to Samuel that his decision was made because he feared the people. Saul's trouble was that he failed to recognize that the God, who had called him, was able to keep him.

Saul had difficulty realizing that the root of his problem was self-centeredness, which stemmed from pride. Though he could have, if he had tried, recognized his shortcoming, he was like a runaway train without any brake. Instead of pausing to resurface from the sea of destruction, in which he was slowly drowning, Saul kept diving deeper and deeper until, alas, he got to the place of no return.

As I studied, carefully, the life of King Saul, I could not help the overwhelming feeling of sorrow that filled my heart. Yes, indeed, God did not desire a king for Israel, as *He* wanted to remain their only king. Despite that fact, they asked for a king, and of all persons, Saul was chosen. He was elevated to a place of prestige and power. God saw in him what he did not see in himself. The prophet Samuel was assigned to anoint him, and considering that mammoth task, in those days, Saul should have fully understood that this was divine. Even the way God ordained him from the onset was proof that he was not meant to be ordinary.

Despite this high calling, Saul kept plummeting deeper and deeper into depravity. When we slip from underneath the umbrella of God's directive, we become easy prey to the devil. Saul was never the same after he disobeyed God. He sunk, never to rise again, and in the end, we read of an anointed king who lost the anointing and whose sin led to idolatry, witchcraft, and then suicide.

My friend, whoever you are, here's my advice to you, stay authentic to your anointing. Do not be a men pleaser! Do not strive to pacify humanity while displeasing God. Whatever He has called you to do, do it!

My friends, today I pray you keep your eyes upon Jesus. If God has called you, *He* will keep you. Aim to please *Him*, and those that belong to *Him* will be pleased with you!

My friend, please understand that you are already defeated if you listen to satan's lies. Stand fast and be not deceived. Whatever a man sows, that's what he will reap.

> Do not be deceived: God cannot be mocked. A man reaps what he sows. Whoever sows to please their flesh, from the flesh will reap destruction; whoever sows to please the Spirit, from the Spirit will reap eternal life. Let us not become weary in doing good, for at the proper

time we will reap a harvest if we do not give up.
(Galatians 6:7–9)

Declaration

I am a soldier of the Lord's army! I am called to serve, and I shall do so with enthusiasm and resilience. I will guard my anointing well! By God's grace, I will never run away from my post.

EMBRACE THE REGENERATED YOU!

Christ bore the believer's sins, and they cannot be charged to him again. Just as in a civil court, if you break the law and pay the penalty for it, the judge cannot charge you for it again. If after you have been sentenced or charged and you are set free, however, you should break the same or another law, you will be considered guilty of a crime again and punished.

In the same manner, a sinner converted is now a new creature, old things are passed away, and behold all things have become new. He has a brand-new slate and is free to walk as a liberated person. There is, therefore, now no condemnation to them that are in Christ Jesus. Another way to put this is, "There is, therefore, no condemnation to them that are regenerated." Such a person is now free to walk in the newness of life. He can no longer be judged by his past life, and those that are mature in Christ fully understand this reality.

What happens, however, if this new creation reverts to his old way of living? We say the old Adamic nature has set in. We say he is now like a dog that goes back to his vomit, and a pig to his wallow (Proverbs 26:11, 2 Peter 2:22). So what does this mean? Well, from the fall of Adam, every person born inherited his sinful nature. I like the way David says it: "*Behold*, I was shaped in iniquity; and in sin did my *mother conceive* me" (Psalm 51:5). That means, before accepting Christ as personal Lord and Savior, every human being has the devil's possessions, which includes demons within. According to scripture, when the demonic spirit is cast out of a man, it goes wondering looking for a new occupant or person within which to live. Remember spirits cannot occupy nonliving things. If it finds no one ready to accommodate or house it, it returns searching for the one from which it was cast. If it sees behavior traits or anything looking like the qualities that attracted it to that person in the first place, it (laughs and) goes looking for seven more spirits that are worse than itself (Matthew 12:43–45). Why is that? It is now ready for overpowering and reoccupying. It doesn't want to be cast out again, right, and the more is the merrier. More means a greater and more powerful hold (stronghold). This person, now possessed by eight spirits, becomes a worse being than he was initially.

Oh, let me remind us that spirits replicate themselves by inviting more overtime. It's possible for a person to be possessed by thousands of spirits (see demoniac of Gadarene in Luke 8:26–39). This person then becomes a reckless and wretched sinner, nonetheless a very hurting one. That is why some backsliders become so devious and obnoxious (Hebrews 6:4–6). They are operating under the influence of several familiar spirits. They literally cannot help themselves! They often want to stop doing what they are doing, but except for the intervention of the Holy Ghost and fire (the language demons understand and fear), they continue in the web spun by satan. They become helpless and sometimes hopeless and, like hardened criminals, destroy many alongside themselves.

Some of these people become ruthless for satan and die in their sins (Philippians 3:19). That is why we must develop bowels of compassion because it's only God's grace that can keep us saved. That's why we must be conscious of and shun the very appearance of evil.

What should the above mean to you and I? Repentance and a constant resistance of sins have to be a daily part of our lives. We must continue to wage war against evil. The reason for this is because we will be punished if we continue to practice the sin for which Christ died, and we have been forgiven. If it's okay for us to continue in sin, wouldn't Christ's death be unprofitable? Why does *He* admonish us to mortify the deeds of the flesh? Why does *He* warn us to die daily? For sure, *He* is not speaking about suicide here! Let's not walk in ignorance, my friends, but enjoy new life in the spirit.

Hello, friend, we aren't saved by good works but are expected to do good works when we are saved. Speaking in tongues doesn't save us, but we are in liberty hall when we are saved, and sometimes we'll run the aisle and speak in tongues. What am I saying? Let's allow the beauty of Jesus to be seen in us, and let's shine for him. Let's walk in the Light, for *He* is the Light.

Please don't take my word for it, friends. Read for yourself! These are just a few of the supporting scriptures that you may find beneficial:

Proverbs 26:11
2 Peter 2:22
Psalm 51:5, 58:3
Ephesians 4:22
Romans 5:12, 6:6, 8:8
Colossians 3:5, 9
Galatians 5:19
1 Corinthians 15:33–34
Genesis 5:3
John 3:6–7

> For ye were sometimes darkness, but now are ye light in the LORD: walk as children of light: (For the fruit of the Spirit is in all goodness and righteousness and truth;) Proving what is acceptable unto the LORD. And have no fellowship with the unfruitful works of darkness, but rather reprove them. For it is a shame even to speak of those things which are done of them in secret. But all things that are reproved are made manifest by the light: for whatsoever doth make manifest is light. Wherefore he saith, Awake thou that sleepest, and arise from the dead, and Christ shall give thee light. (Ephesians 5:8–14)

Declaration

Today I embrace the truth of who I am and to whom I belong. I choose to walk in the light since my deeds are not evil! I will be who God has called me to become in Jesus' name! Amen.

RISE ABOVE FEAR

Hello there, friend, I know that, like myself, you thought that fear was merely human's reaction to situations over which they feel they have no control. That is what many people suggest, but did you know that fear is a demonic spirit? Did you also know that faith is a gift as well as a fruit from God?

While the average person may think it's okay to be fearful sometimes or most times, God is not okay with us being afraid. Contrary to what may be deduced, fear indicates a lack of faith in God. Fear shows that we doubt *His* ability to handle the troubles that face us! Fear would not be such a dreadful thing if it didn't paralyze us so severely. When we become fearful, we go into panic mode. Panic shifts our godly equilibrium. When this happens, we are plunged into an abyss of desperation. This deviates us from God's help because most times, when we become fearful, we don't remember to pray.

Fear is not limited to any one individual. Please understand that I am in no way saying I have not had fears, but I've had to, and I am still learning to deal with them. The truth is, to counteract fear, my faith level has to shift every time. It must become superior to the fear that's seeking to overpower me. Through the word of God, I've come to realize that when I'm afraid, I give my authority to the devil. When I act through fear and allow panic to set in, I'm also making myself lord over my situation, thus telling God *He's* not able to help me.

God doesn't want us to be afraid because He wants us to trust *Him*. *He* wants us to have total confidence and know that *He* can help us through any circumstance in our lives.

The spirit of fear operates similarly to a dog. Do you own one or know anything at all about dogs? As far back as I can recall, I've always had them, mainly watchdogs (except for right now). Dogs are incredible animals that know when to run and when to fight. If they sense fear from you, even those that are typically submissive become aggressive toward you! Yes, they will if they know you are afraid.

Because dogs are experts at reading body language, they can quickly pick up on someone who is scared of them. They can smell fear. When we are afraid, sweat glands are more active, producing *body odor* a dog can smell. There's even evidence that dogs can see fear as well as other emotions on our face. However, our body language sends the strongest and most significant signal to a dog. People who are afraid of dogs often stare at them, which the dog interprets as confrontational. Instead of staying calm, a fearful person will tense up, which also tells the dog this person wants to fight. Someone who is afraid of dogs will likely have no idea what a dog's body language means; therefore, their body language may be telling the dog all the wrong things. A fearful person can put a dog in a defensive state of mind.

Well, you ask, what does fear for dogs have to do with this discussion? Need I tell you, friend? Like dogs, the devil knows when we're afraid. Unlike dogs, however, he doesn't need to smell because he's able to hear through our words and tell by our actions and behavior that we are afraid. He notices how we get from a place of confidence to a place of confinement and cowardice. He observes, and then he comes in for the kill. Unlike when we face a dog, we must become confrontational when the devil approaches. If we cower, he becomes excited, and that's when all hell gets into action. Like a killer whale that smells blood, the devil then comes in like a flood to steal, kill, and destroy!

Friends, in this season, I implore you, be wise and trust God like never before. Kill every fear with faith. Use the word of God! Speak to every diabolic spirit with all the authority you can muster. Pray and release the fire of God. Trust God, knowing that *He* will not disappoint you.

Allow yourself to exercise faith over fear as you recognize that nothing can be against you if God is for you.

> There is no fear in love; but perfect love casteth out fear: because fear hath torment. He that feareth is not made perfect in love. (1 John 4:18)

Declaration

I am as bold as a lion. I embrace and walk in love, power, and a sound mind!

BRUISED TO BLESS!

Hello there, friend, while the region, time, technique, technology, type of grapes and wines that are desired may vary, the process in every wine harvest includes but is not limited to these basic vine-to-wine steps:

1. Picking the grapes
2. Crushing the grapes
3. Fermenting the grapes into wine
4. Aging the wine
5. Bottling the wine

Sure enough, most people love wine, whether it is the nonalcoholic one, which usually has less than 0.5 percent alcohol, the alcohol-free wine which contains 0 percent alcohol, or the regular wine. Indeed, its consumption is necessary for many wine lovers worldwide because it adds flavour to food. While there are myriads of wines, the wine-making process is uniquely similar for most part.

When grapes are picked, they must be crushed for the juice to be removed from them. Crushing the grapes is a very straightforward task. It's simply a matter of breaking or bursting grape berries and allowing the juice, pulp, and seeds to mingle with the skins and stems of the grapes. On the other hand, pressing separates the grape juice from the fibre and other solids that make up a berry. Sometimes, crushing and pressing are done at the same time, though they can be separated by a few hours or days, depending on the type of wine being made.

So why have I mentioned this wine-making process, my friend? Yes, you got it right, because like wine, we must be crushed, bruised, and often battered for a couple of reasons.

Our bruising is in and of itself a gift of grace because as we are broken, pride and high thoughts are levelled. During the bruising and the battering stages of our lives, we are exposed to our inadequacies and insufficiency. In fact, during this season, we get an excellent opportunity to better understand that we indeed are frail and helpless by nature. My friend, as painful as this truth is, I must tell you that we both need bruising so that we will know who we are, lean on our heavenly Father, and not attempt to lean on our own understanding.

At the risk of you disagreeing with me, for now until the Holy Spirit reveals to you what I am saying, I will shock you further by saying that bruising is what helps us to recognize that we must live by mercy. That is, we need God's mercy, and we must, in turn, extend understanding.

Another reality is that if grapes are not bruised and squeezed, they will not produce wine. Had I not been bruised and a few times too many crushed, I would not recognize my gift, thus, allowing you to be holding this book. You see, my friend, what you might not know is that this book is written from experience. As sophisticated as it may appear, this is not a feel-good book. I didn't write it because I got a dream. I wrote it from a place of experience. I have now learnt to thank God for trials as they have made me more resilient. I have grown wiser because of my bruising. I have become a better person because I didn't allow bruising to make me bitter. I chose to be better and become a blessing.

Right now, I encourage you to let the bruises of life make you a blessing and not a bitter snob. No matter what storm you have just experienced, are experiencing, or will experience, please know that joy awaits. You must live it before you can describe it. You will be stronger for it! You will be better! If you allow yourself to heal, you will be the biggest asset in someone's life. You are meant to shine, rise above the bruising, and become a blessing. If you are already there, it's for a cause, hold on. Jesus will see you through.

But he *was* wounded for our transgressions, *he was* bruised for our iniquities: the chastisement of our peace *was* upon him; and with his stripes we are healed. (Isaiah 53:5)

Declaration

I will joy in my sorrow because I understand that I am being bruised to bless. I will trust the process and wear a crown someday!

TURN YOUR WEEPING INTO WORSHIP

To weep is to express grief, sorrow, or any overpowering emotion by crying or shedding tears. In some instances, persons weep with joy, but on most occasions, weeping is associated with sorrow.

The word *weep* (or *wept*, its past tense) is used in the Bible from Genesis to Revelation at least eighty-two times. The Bible clearly shows weeping occurring from people fearing death, experiencing the death of loved ones, as they escaped troubles, as they encountered problems, as they were faced by fiery trials, in the presence of Jesus, outside the presence of Jesus, and the list continues.

Of all the weeping mentioned in the scriptures, the ones that stand out the most to me are those which indicated that Jesus wept. He wept at the grave of Lazarus—as he looked on and saw the unbelief of the Jewish people who failed to recognize his lordship over death and the grave (John 11:35). Jesus wept when he looked on and recalled the pending catastrophe that would occur in that beloved city of Jerusalem (Luke 19:41–44). He also cried in the days of his flesh when he had offered up prayers and supplications with strong crying and tears unto him that was able to save him from death and was heard in that He feared (Hebrews 5:7).

Jesus' weeping is indicative that, like us, though fully God, He was fully man and had all capabilities to feel and be affected by human situations. In other words, Jesus, as God in the flesh, revealed the truth that *He* became a man in the first place, so that He could die on the cross (Philippians 2:5–8). But He also became a man so that He could be touched with the feeling of our infirmities (Hebrews 4:15–16). Yes, He also became flesh so that we could touch Him!

My friends, if Jesus, as well as other characters in the Bible, wept, please know that you too will cry. Perhaps, you are faced with a trying situation that has reduced you to bitter tears. Maybe you are currently at a Red Sea that seems uncrossable. You may feel overwhelmed with sorrow. It may appear as if all odds are against you and that God has forsaken you. Perhaps you are weeping even as you read this book. Perhaps, your puffy eyes are reminders of the anger, bitterness, sorrow, and grief that have assailed you in recent times. Yes, friend, you may be weeping, but God wants to turn your weeping to worship. He wants you to rise above the pains of the past and give Him the glory, which belongs to Him.

There's power in crying, but to whom are you crying? If you aren't crying unto God, you're wasting your tears!

Hear me and hear me well, friend, the devil will never cringe at your tears. He is strengthened by pity and enjoys tears. He is highly turned on when he smells fear and doubt and sees tears, at least when these tears are helpless.

Do you know that even your friends break down when you cry helplessly, and at other times, they are revolted and repulsed by it? Why is that? Some people do not know how to deal with the tears of others. All in all, tears are chiefly useful and beneficial when you go before God in worship or prayer.

You've often heard that tears are languages that God understands, is that true? Of course, because *He* is God, Father of all lives, and when you have a very personal relationship with *Him*, *He* becomes your very own *Abba*. So before you speak, *He* knows your thoughts. In fact, *God* knew all you'd be thinking for this entire day before you woke this morning. He already knows what you'll be thinking tomorrow and for all your allotted days on this earth. So guess what, friend? He knows when you're sad, cast down, and the whole works. He even knew what would cause you the pain you may now be experiencing before you were born and even became an adult or are at your current age.

Do you think *He* was joking when *He* said, "Come unto me, all ye that labour and are heavy laden and I will give you rest. Take my yoke upon you, and learn of me; for I am meek and lowly in heart: and ye shall find rest unto your souls"? (Matthew 11:28–29).

He doesn't want you to stay in a place of pain, but *He* knows someday you'll experience pain. That's why *He* said come unto me. Don't try everything else before seeking Him who has given the most beautiful invitation? *He* is as real as you make *Him* in your life.

As I write to you now, *He's* within me and also around me. He surrounds me. *He is* real. I feel *Him. I hear Him. I'm comforted by Him all the time. He* can be your *Abba* too.

He is the only one who cares enough and can help you. Of course, therapy helps, and counselling is good, but what's next? Are they working? Be honest with me. How many times have you heard of the side effects of antidepressants? Don't you know that stress medication causes hangovers? You may not know much about antidepressants, but what about the different things to which you are addicted? Perhaps it's food to which you turn when you are depressed. Maybe it's wines or beers! Whatever you are addicted to, you can turn away from it and turn to Jesus. That is how your weeping will turn to worship.

Go to God in prayer and be honest with *Him* today. What if you should lock yourself into your room, go on your face, and call *Him*? Don't you think *He'll* come? Do you know you can tell *Him* your darkest secrets? Are you asking why? Okay, let me tell you, *He* knows all about you. It doesn't matter how anointed you are. It doesn't matter how gifted and extraordinary you appear to the world. It doesn't matter that you think you are the only one who knows what you did last night, *God* knows. *He* knew you would go there, do that, say that, and behave that way. *He* knew before you acted. So if that's the case, why don't you confess it to *Him*? When you cry to your friends or merely sit in your room, cry, smoke pot and cigarette, drink some alcohol, and engage in loose sex, what happens next? There's the guilt, possible unwanted pregnancy, STD or STI, and myriad of other distresses that satan never tells you about.

Get into worship overdrive, my friend; step out of the natural and into the supernatural. Do not allow the storms of life and the circumstances sent your way to defeat you. Worship Him whom your soul loves. Let go of yourself and worship the God who is more than enough and altogether lovely. Humble yourself before God, surrender every part of your life to His control and ruler-ship. Go past praising Him. Praise is paying homage for what God has done, but when you worship, you reverence Him for who He is.

My friend, worship is a lifestyle, not an occasional activity. Jesus said, "*The Father is seeking those who will worship Him in spirit and truth*" (John 4:23), "*Worship the Lord in the beauty of holiness*" (Psalm 96:9), and "*Come let us worship and bow down*" (Psalm 95:6). Be humble and contrite before Him so the Holy Spirit can speak to you, convict you, and comfort you. Worship God so you can realign your priorities with His and acknowledge Him as the Lord of your life.

Remember now, my friend. Praise is not the same as worship. Praise is intertwined with thanksgiving. Worship is intertwined with surrender. You cannot worship God and another at the same time (Luke 4:8). Bowing down, kneeling before Him, lifting holy hands—these help to create the necessary attitude of humility required for real worship.

Worship God, my friend. Come on now, give Him the highest praise. Shout hallelujah to our King. It is the highest praise. Confuse the enemy! He expects you to crumble; he expects you to buckle under the pressure. My sister, my brother, satan knows that weeping often causes us to lose focus. He wants to distract you. How about bowing to your *King* and paying homage to Him.

Whatever season you are experiencing right now, friend, whatever storm clouds are hanging low, understand that you are endowed with the grace and capacity to make it to the other side.

Thou hast turned for me my mourning into dancing: thou hast put off my sackcloth, and girded me with gladness. (Psalm 30:11)

Declaration

Today I accept beauty for ashes and strength for fear. I exchange mourning for gladness and peace for despair!

BEATING FAILURE IN THE SECOND ROUND

What is failure? How is it measured? The answers to these questions vary from person to person, but of one thing I am sure—all people will agree that failure is not a good thing. There is such a stigma attached to this dreaded word that many have had to seek therapy once they have had such an experience.

Is failure the end of the road though? Is it possible to catapult into success after experiencing one or several bouts of failure?

I am sure that you know Hershey's chocolate, but do you know the story behind it or its manufacturer? According to history, when Milton Hershey first started his candy production career, he was a nobody. After being fired from an apprenticeship with a printer, Hershey started three separate candy-related ventures and was forced to watch all of them fail.

In one last attempt, Hershey founded the Lancaster Caramel Company and started seeing tremendous results. Believing in his vision for milk chocolate for the masses, he eventually founded the Hershey Company and became one of the most well-known names in the industry.

While Hershey is a good illustration, why don't we take a closer look at a famous Bible character that beat failure in the second round? This guy's name is Moses.

If he lived in our time, he would likely be branded as an insecure, exile loser. In fact, in my opinion, Moses suffered from extremely low self-esteem and showed a lack of self-confidence. He was so unwilling to cooperate and showed such cowardice from all the excuses he gave that God was tempted to kill him at one point. Can you imagine Moses saying to God, "I can't do what you want me to do because I have a terrible, horrible past, I've sinned, I killed, I lied, I ran away, I betrayed my family's confidence, I relinquished my spiritual talents, I'm full of hate, and worst of all, I stutter." Bear in mind, those were only some of the excuses Moses had.

The book of Exodus gives a vivid description of Moses's insecurities and failures. Overall, we can safely say that he was plagued by his identity problems, needed some anger management classes, started his political career by killing an opponent, then ran away to hide from everyone, including God. Despite all his activities, we can safely say that there was undoubtedly a specific calling on Moses's life. He felt it, he knew it, but though well learnt in Egypt, he was never taught about a sovereign God who has his own time and place for everything, including our calling and dreams and for when all of them will happen and come true.

Like Moses, you may know there is a living God and may even be resentful of the system of life that faces you, your family, and even your society. You may want a better life for your people, but your trust may be in your human skills like him. Even now, you may be as down and out as Moses first was. Maybe, you are hiding due to a life of promiscuity and wantonness. You may be a marriage wrecker or be in a wrecked marriage. Perhaps, you are simply a good person who is rebelling and doing your best to rise again due to past mistakes and misgivings.

That's okay. There is hope for you because even eighty years of rising and falling was not sufficient to break Moses to God's will and way!

He was filled with uncertainties, but there was a round two for him, amid all his obvious failing. Moses had removed himself from the Egyptian community and lifestyle to the lonely and exile lifestyle. This might have taken some getting used to, but it was here, in the worst place ever, unsure of who he was anymore, and with a feeling of being far from his calling (as a loser) that he had a "remove your shoes" experience in the presence of the true God.

Moses had many excuses, but God, the creator of perseverance, had an uncanny plan for him. God himself insisted on Moses calling and assured him that if he kept his faith and believed, he would lead the people of Israel out of slavery.

My friend, before it got better for Milton Hershey and Moses, it got worse, but guess what, they beat failure in the second round.

What should you do at this point? That's easier said than done, but it is possible: Draw inspiration from Milton and Moses. The next time you experience failure, no matter the magnitude, hold your head up, square your shoulder, and let that devil know, "I will beat failure in the second round."

Sure, sometimes failures seems like the end of the road, but remember, many successful men and women in the world today are in such position because they decided to push past the inevitable bleakness of failure.

Learn from your mistakes, reflect and accept the loss, but revisit your passion and keep pursuing your goals no matter what.

> Rejoice not against me, O mine enemy:
> when I fall, I shall arise; when I sit in darkness,
> the LORD *shall be* a light unto me. (Micah 7:8)

Declaration

The joy of the Lord is my strength. Today, I take all necessary steps of faith to make my journey successful. I can do all things through Christ, who gives me the power to act.

"SPEAK THE WORD," EVERY WALL MUST FALL

A *battle* or *war cry* is a word or phrase shouted by soldiers of the same combatant as they go into battle. Although one purpose of this cry is to invoke patriotic sentiment—that is, getting soldiers to maintain belief in the goal of their country and army in the face of opposition or hardship—the chief is to arouse hostility, thus causing the opposing army to become intimidated. In essence, battle cries are sometimes so formidable that the enemy, preferring to avoid confrontation, opts to flee. To emphasize aggression, battle cries need to be as loud as possible. Historically, acoustic devices such as horns, drums, conches, carnyxes, bagpipes, and bugles were used for amplifying sounds.

Having made such an illustration, my friend, my question to you is, "What insurmountable walls surround you right now? What high thing needs to be brought low? What is it that is troubling you in this season? Is it sickness, sorrow, poverty, torment, fear, doubt, or something else? Has it dawned on you that you can speak a word and change your situation?" Oh, friend! Let me ask you an earnest question, "When was the last time that you released a word or a battle cry? Don't you know you can speak a word which causes the enemy to flee?"

In the Scripture, the centurion ruler knew the power of the spoken word, which is why he said to Jesus, "Speak the word only and my servant shall be healed" (Matthew 8:8).

Jesus, upon approaching Lazarus's tomb, shouted his name and commanded him to come forth.

When you are silent, at a time when you need to speak, you are consenting to what is being said or what is happening to you. What I mean is that, when you are in a bad or dissatisfying situation and you remain silent, you are giving the case power to harass you. My friend, there is a time and a season for all things. Certainly, there is a time to speak.

So here is something of which I wish to remind you today: Your word is the most potent force that you possess! Your words have power and energy that can bless or curse, build or destroy, heal or hurt, help or hinder. In short, your word can cause either life or death to occur. Your victory is in your mouth! Hello there, are you listening to what I am saying? You can change any situation, which is happening in your life, simply by speaking a word. Just as a soldier releases battle cries that affect his atmosphere, so it is that you can use your word to change your atmosphere. As the scriptures declare, "By faith, we understand that the *universe* was created by the *word of God*, so that what is seen was made from things that are not visible."

Are you a believer? Do you belong to the *King*? If so, and if you understand Genesis chapter 1, then you should know that your word carries weight. Why is that? You ask, but don't you remember that your heavenly Father used His word to form the earth and all that is in it? The Lord granted us WORD ACCESS POWER when Jesus died on the cross of Calvary. Yes, my friend, there is a time to refrain from talking, but surely, there is a time to speak. The word of a glory carrier is full of power. Open your mouth, *child of God*, and speak to every mountain in your life. If you do, they must crumble to the ground.

> And it shall come to pass, that when they make a long *blast* with the ram's horn, *and* when ye hear the sound of the trumpet, all the people shall shout with a great shout; and the wall of the city shall fall down flat, and the people shall ascend up every man straight before him. So the people shouted when *the priests* blew with

the trumpets: and it came to pass, when the
people heard the sound of the trumpet, and the
people shouted with a great shout, that the wall
fell down flat, so that the people went up into
the city, every man straight before him, and they
took the city. (Joshua 6:5, 20)

Declaration

I know who I am, and I know the weight that my word carries.
Today, I release a missile from my mouth that destroys every wall
erected by the enemy of my soul.

UNDERSTAND THE INSEPARABLE SEPARATION

Hey there, friend, what would you do if you truly understood how well your heavenly Father loves you? Do you know that He is a covenant-keeping God? Are you aware that He says He loves you with an everlasting love? Do you know that His mind is full of you? Are you aware that His greatest desire is to have a deep and long-lasting loving relationship with you?

His love is not the same as a man for a woman or a mother for a child; it is way more profound and stronger. Even though He made all living things, He gives special attention to you. Not a sparrow falls from the sky without His knowledge, and yet you are worth way more than sparrows. His love for you is what prompted Him to number every hair on your head. *He* watches over you day and night, and though you do not always remember or think about Him, His love for you is undying. When all others fail you, He will never forsake you. He will never fail or forget you. I know that some days you wonder if He is real or genuinely cares about you. Oh yes, friend, He cares!

If you desire to understand if God cares for you or not, ask Him. He is not far from them that seek Him. His love is inseparable. His love for you is not based on how good you are. His love for you is not based on the work that you do. He loves and had grand plans for you, long before you were born. His love for you supersedes the most incredible love you will ever experience in this life! His love for you supersedes any love that you could give to Him. He loves you whether you are good or bad. He loves you whether you are happy or sad. His greatest desire, however, is to make you His bride. He wants to form a covenant with you.

A covenant is an agreement, usually formal, between two or more persons to do or not to do something specified. Once this agreement is entered into, all persons involved are expected to keep their end of the bargain. When God enters into a covenant with His children, those who love, trust, and surrender their lives to Him, He never breaks it. Remember, He is not a man that He should lie and the son of man that he should repent or change His mind. If God makes a promise to you, He will keep it until the very end. He will never go back on His word. Faithful is He who has called you, and He will do it. God's love is stronger than death because in life, He loves His own, and after death, they will live and reign with Him. His love is an inseparable separation. His love is not hinged on any person's opinion of you.

My friend, you may have experienced a broken heart in one or more relationships but Jesus is the mender of broken hearts. He specializes in brokenness. His love is so impenetrable that only sin can affect it. Do you know the good news, though, my friend? He is forever married to the backslider. That means, even when someone gets into a relationship with Him and breaks his vow, He still loves and cares for such individual. All this person has to do is keep his end of the bargain, and indeed, all things will become new.

God's love is so genuine, so deep, and so true. It is the best thing that any human being can ever experience.

My friend, once you truly understand this inseparable separation, then you are on your way to true joy, peace, success, and happiness. Would you like to overcome the evil powers of this world's system? Let Christ into your heart, and the things around you will grow strangely dim. There is only one source of pure, divine love, and wherever that love is present, it's clear that the possessor has found its origin in God. God's love is absolutely selfless. He loves the unlovable and teaches them how to love by putting away their sin and perfecting their union with Him. He is a shield and the lifter of the heads of all those who genuinely love, trust, and rely on Him. If you are in a relationship with Him, seek to intensify it. Let nothing separate you from His love. Remember, He will never stop loving and reaching out to you. If you have never known the joy of a beautiful relationship with the Lord Jesus Christ, now is an excellent time to learn the steps for this journey. Now is a good time to embrace a relationship or recommit your life to Him. His arms are wide open, ready to embrace whoever chooses to make a covenant with Him. I'm glad I did. What about you? Wouldst thou overcome the world? Let Christ enter, and the world will have no charms for thee.

> Herein is love, not that we loved God, but that he loved us, and sent his Son [to be] the propitiation for our sins. (1 John 4:10)

Declaration

I connect myself to the true vine. I stand upon the promises of the Lord. I believe that He has great plans for me. Nothing shall separate me from His love.

SOME WHO COME CAN'T GO WITH YOU

Hello there, friend. How are you doing? As we traverse the journey called life, we meet different people and have various experiences. These individuals all play a significant role and help to shape our lives in some way. At times we become friends with some of these folks, and they become essential. They become so relevant to us that they influence many of our choices. Whether we acknowledge it or not, a lot of the decisions we make result from the people to whom we open ourselves. Their opinion counts, and these lead to us making certain choices or decisions. Of course, some of these decisions are good and have helped to shape our lives positively. Others are bad and have caused us many heartaches and pains.

Yes, we are social beings who fully comprehend that no man is an island and no man stands alone. It is for this very cause that we seek to form relationships.

When this happens, we trust and believe that nothing can sever the ties that bind our hearts together. What we are generally never prepared for is when ties are cut. Oh yes, it is a painful feat and causes significant shifts in our equilibrium. For some people, separations can be so great that it leads to traumatic experiences. Many persons have even ended their lives because of a broken heart caused by someone they deeply loved. Many persons have suffered mental breakdowns, loss of trust, and grave illnesses due to relationships that failed over time.

The problem is that we ignore the word of God. Many scriptures have warned about the fleetingness of man's love. It indicates, quite clearly, that we should not put our trust in humankind. Instead, we should place all our confidence in God. Yes, we must love. Yes, we must seek relationship but never love the creature more than the creator.

Many persons fail to recognize that true love is only found in God. A person has to be full of God to be capable of true love because God is love. Indeed, no matter how we start a journey with a person, he or she may not be around in the long run.

Of course, separation is not always intentional, neither is the person who leaves us when we need them the most, consistently doing this of their own accord. God often removes someone from our lives because they do not fit into the plan that He has for us. I have learnt that people come into our lives for a reason, a season, or a lifetime, and I agree. It means, therefore, that when people come along, we must understand their purpose. Of course, many times, we discover their purpose very late. Regrettably, we also try to hold on to them when we need to set them free. We soon recognize that the moment they left was the moment when we indeed began to soar.

My friend, not everyone who starts a journey with you will be there at the end. This is one truth with which you must make peace. The moment you can accept this, you can enjoy greater peace of mind and true happiness. It's worth fighting for some relationships, with every breath you possess, but some are not. Sometimes, you must open your fingers, hold out your hands, and let it go. Learning to grasp earthly things loosely and holding firmly to Jesus Christ is the key to living well. Not all who come can go with you!

> And Abram went up out of Egypt, he, and his wife, and all that he had, and Lot with him, into the south. And Abram said unto Lot, Let there be no strife, I pray thee, between me and thee, and between my herdsmen and thy herdsmen; for we be brethren. Is not the whole land before thee? Separate thyself, I pray thee, from me: if thou wilt take the left hand, then I will go to the right; or if thou depart to the right hand, then I will go to the left. (Genesis 13:1, 8–9)

Declaration

I recognize that life is fleeting and filled with uncertainties. I am cognizant that not all who starts the journey of life with me will be at my side at the finish line. I will, therefore, hold all earthly things loosely and hold fast to Jesus Christ!

YOU WILL SING THE VICTOR'S SONG

A winner isn't so called until he has accomplished a particular task. A winner is not one who has never lost a battle but is one who stays the course until victory is won. Indeed, as we navigate life, we will be lent many blows, but what we must understand is that for every blow through which we stand and for every victory that we win, we become stronger.

It is true that life can sometimes be daunting and challenging. There are many valleys in which we must precariously trod and many mountains over which we must climb. Indeed, the path is frequently winding and there are precipices over which we dare not fall. Yes, it's true, friend, that getting to the other side, the side of victory, is not easy, but likewise, not impossible. On many occasions, we will fall and experience cuts and bruises.

You have been rightly told that life is not a bed of roses. The unfailing reality, however, is that there is no situation into which we find ourselves, which we cannot escape. All we need to do is to put our trust and confidence in the one who is known to calm the storm. At times, life throws such boisterous blows that we are confident that we will not make it, at least alive. Sometimes we experience pains, lack, heartaches, grief, and sorrow, but we must never give up. We must understand that everything has a time and a season under the heavens.

It is true that at times, we will become overwhelmed and even alarmed based on the circumstances of life that face us, but if our eyes are upon the hills, from whence cometh our help, and if we remember that even when we walk through the valley of the shadow of death, he is with us, we will win.

My friend, there is a song that is reserved for winners. It is, however, never sung at the middle of the race, but at the finish line.

If you are currently faced with a situation that seems impossible and your head is hanging low, rest assured in the reality that you will smile again, once you stay your course. If you get to the end of the race, you will sing the winner's anthem, and best of all, those who see the eagle within you and await you at the finish line will join you in singing the *victor's* song. It may not be easy right now, my friend. It may seem as if you are barely able to put one foot in front of the other, but keep going, keep trusting, because victory shall be your portion, in Jesus's name!

> Blessed is the man that endures temptation:
> for when he is tried, he shall receive the crown of
> life, which the Lord hath promised to them that
> love him. (James 1:12)

Declaration

I am victorious through the blood of Jesus, Jesus Christ! I am made to prevail over every situation. I shall finish my course with strength and agility.

THE STORM IS OVER

The world watched in horror as the hurricane lashed the country full force. It was like a mad giant that was determined to destroy all in view. The year was 2013 and was known as the one that caused the most massive humanitarian crisis in the country's history. Around four thousand people were confirmed dead in the aftermath of the typhoon, with thousands more still unaccounted for. As devastating as that storm was, the sad fact was that it was nowhere near the deadliest storm to have struck Asia. One of its most horrific was Cyclone Nargis. With gusting *winds* of up to 164 kilometers per hour, it marched ashore, bringing with it a monster storm surge that reached far inland, up along the low-lying and densely populated Irrawaddy Delta. More than 140,000 lives were lost in the year 2008.

That sounds familiar right, friend? Storms are deadly, and they are devastating. They destroy lives, property, and dreams. Much depression and confusion are the aftermath of a storm. The thing I want to tell you, however, is that as devastating as a storm is, it has duration. No matter how boisterous and overwhelming it is, there is always a lull. No storm lasts forever. Yes, during its course, it seems as though it will never end, but in the fullness of time, it must end!

Today, as you turn the final pages of this book, I know undoubtedly that you have seen your fair share of storms. I know that you have had boisterous and windy situations that drove you many times to your knees. Indeed, there were times when you were so overwhelmed that you had no idea where to turn or to whom to run. Truly the pressures of life have beaten against your frame in the form of sicknesses, lack, shame, pain, sorrow, and low self-esteem. You may have even been plagued by countless days, months, and even years of secret pains, addictions, doubts, and fears. So many times you may have felt as though you wouldn't make it, but look at you now! Child of God, look into your mirror. You have weathered the storm, and now you are a formidable force. As promised, God has been your keeper. He has been your very present help. He will never lead you into a storm that He doesn't give you the power to overcome. Mark this truth down, friend, *no storm lasts forever*!

As my time draws to a close with you in this season, here is a point of reminder: What distinguishes those who are overpowered by life from those who rule in life is the knowledge that battles and conflicts are inevitable; however unlike the person who doesn't know God, His children have power over whatever may come against them. So they can, and must, fight relentlessly until the battle is won.

If at any time you feel as though the waves and the wind are storming around you, stand fast and remember that your heavenly Father is on your boat. Let that truth saturate and permeate every fiber of your being today and always. If you haven't yet made the Peace Speaker your Lord and Master, now is a good time to do so. See Mark 16:16 and Acts 2:38.

> Now thanks *be* unto God, which always causes us to triumph in Christ, and makes manifest the savour of his knowledge by us in every place. (2 Corinthians 2:14)

Declaration

Nothing lasts forever! Today I stand in awe of the amazing grace of the Lord of Glory! Today, with a triumphant shout, I say, "All praise be unto the Lord Most High, my refuge and very present help in times of trouble!"

CONCLUSION

My friend, it has indeed been a fantastic journey with you. I wish you God's choicest blessings. Be well until we meet again! Shalom.

ABOUT THE AUTHOR

Doreen Moore-Barrett is a child of Jesus Christ! She is pretty frank but possesses great intrinsic value. She can be approached by any individual who will leave her presence feeling refreshed, restored, and renewed. A teacher by profession, she hails from the beautiful isles of the West Indies. Awarded twice for excellence in education, Doreen has stalwartly served in various capacities in the National Teachers' Association body. She facilitated new interns for several years and district president for all schools in her district.

She is a certified health and family life coordinator and a poet. Despite serving in many strata—regionally and internationally— Doreen understands that she is first called to represent her *King* and *Savior—Jesus Christ*. This she does with great humility and sobriety. She is the wife of, one husband, Levi Barrett, whom she loves completely. She has served in various ministerial capacities such as missionary, regional prayer coordinator, Sunday school director, assistant youth president, adult Sunday school teacher to name a few. Mrs. Moore-Barrett has served on many committees, as she continues to draw her strength from the Lord. She is indebted to God for His mercies, grace, and continued favours. When Doreen is not writing, she is praying, studying, or reading. In her spare time, she enjoys crocheting, doing "find a word" puzzles, and listening to soothing worship music.

Look for her next book, which will be released very soon!

CPSIA information can be obtained
at www.ICGtesting.com
Printed in the USA
BVHW060043300322
632824BV00009B/490

9 781685 179946